J
ENCYCLOPEDIA

Animal Kingdom

STERLING

JUNIOR ENCYCLOPEDIA

Animal Kingdom

STERLING

STERLING

Sterling Publishers Private Limited

A-59, Okhla Ind. Area, Phase II, New Delhi-110020. India
Tel: 91-11-26386165; Fax: 91-11-26383788
E-mail: mail@sterlingpublishers.com
Website: www.sterlingpublishers.com

Junior Encyclopedia - Animal Kingdom
© 2011, Sterling Publishers Private Limited

All rights are reserved. No part of this publication may be reproduced, stored in a retrieval system or transmitted, in any form or by any means, mechanical, photocopying, recording or otherwise, without prior written permission of the publisher.

Printed at Sterling Publishers Pvt. Ltd, New Delhi

Contents

Introduction	11
Vertebrates	12
Birds	13
Mammals	59
Reptiles	102
Amphibians	131
Marine Animals	143
Invertebrates	180
Extinct, Endangered Species and Conservation	200

Introduction

The animal world extends from the large open spaces of grasslands to the icy Polar Regions; from the warm rainforests to the depth of the oceans. Animals dwell in all corners of the world - wetlands, islands, coral reefs, forests and deserts. There are almost two million species recorded to date that are living on this earth, each one having vast differences from the next. More are yet to be discovered.

This book tells you of the weird and wonderful world of animals, some that you already know of and others that you never knew existed, some that move swiftly and stealthily and some whose movement is slow and lumbering. From the different habitats that they inhabit to the different kinds of food that they eat, together, they all make up our animal kingdom.

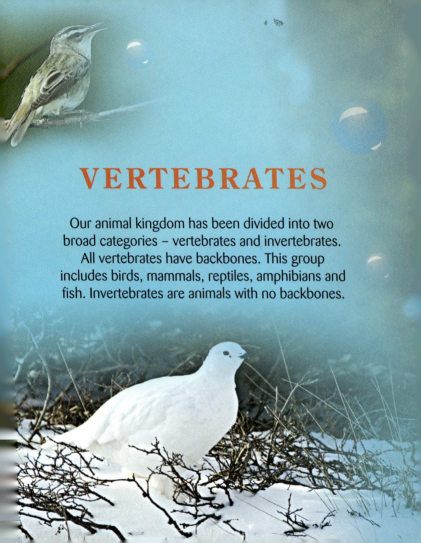

VERTEBRATES

Our animal kingdom has been divided into two broad categories – vertebrates and invertebrates. All vertebrates have backbones. This group includes birds, mammals, reptiles, amphibians and fish. Invertebrates are animals with no backbones.

Bird

Whether they fly or not, what makes birds one of a kind is that they have feathers. No other animal has feathers. Instead of teeth, they have bills which help them to feed. In common with other vertebrates, they do have a backbone and like mammals they are warm-blooded—the temperature of their body does not vary with the temperature outside.

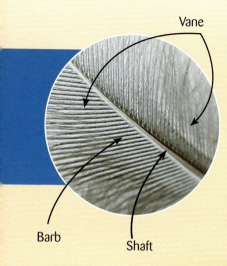

Vane

Barb

Shaft

The Main Feature: Feathers

Generally, feathers are of two kinds: contour feathers and down feathers. Contour feathers are large and help birds to fly, down feathers are small and fluffy, keeping them warm.

Feathers have a central shaft and its two sides are called vanes. The branches on each vane are called barbs and these barbs have further small branches called barbules.

Feathered Fiend

The fierce and meat-eating Velociraptors, the raptors we saw in Jurassic Park might actually have been covered in feathers (would they have looked silly then?)! That is because they could have formed an in-between stage in evolution between dinosaurs and birds.

Why Humans Cannot Fly and Birds Can

The bones of birds are hollow so that they are light and are able to fly. On, the other hand, the reason humans cannot fly is that they are heavy and their muscles don't have the strength to lift them up. The quick rate at which a bird's heart pumps blood allows them to flap their wings. Whereas a human heart only has 60 to 80 beats a minute, a sparrow's heart can beat 800 times a minute!

Too Close for Comfort

In Greek myth, Daedalus, a master craftsman and his son Icarus were imprisoned in the palace of the King of Crete. Daedalus made two pairs of wings out of wax for both of them and flew. Daedalus warned his son not to fly too close to the sun, but Icarus was so thrilled about flying that he flew near it. The wax in his wings melted and he fell into the sea.

A Bird's Eye View

Birds have sharper eyesight than us humans. From a height of 100 feet, the American Kestrel can zero in on its prey, say a poor grasshopper, and swoop down till it grabs it, without losing its focus even once. As for different distances, birds can adjust their focus to see clearly much faster than animals.

Eagle Eyes

An eagle can stare into the sun. And that is because, like all birds, they have a transparent third eyelid called the nictitating membrane. Instead of going up and down, it moves from left to right. It also saves the eyes of owls from the harsh rays of the sun.

Migration

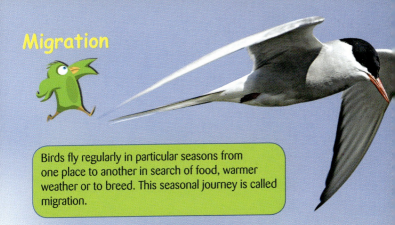

Birds fly regularly in particular seasons from one place to another in search of food, warmer weather or to breed. This seasonal journey is called migration.

Extra Energy

For sedge warblers, doubling their weight and adding a lot of extra fat is a good thing. This is because they need the energy from it to fly without stopping from Europe to Africa, that is, 3000 to 4000 km in three to four days.

The Sad Swallow

Being only 20 grams in weight, the swallow has to travel a distance of 10,000 km. In the course of this, on an average, half the adults and eighty percent of the young die.

Eurasian Cuckoo

Female Eurasian Cuckoos migrate after they have laid their eggs in another birds' nest. When these hatch, the young ones already know the migration route their real parents have taken and fly 4,500 to 12,000 km a month later to their parents' location!

To Nest...

With only their beaks, their feet and with what's around them, birds put in a lot of hard work to build the most unique nests.

'Real' Estate

Weaverbirds build complex nests out of grass or leaf strips. Large community nests are woven out of grass in trees by the social weavers of Africa. While parents live in their own 'apartments', the young keep adding new ones. If you look at it from a distance, it looks like the hatched roof of a human hut!

Titanic Nests

The largest nest any bird has is that of the bald eagle's. It uses it for a long time and keeps adding building material over the years. It can be as large as 4m deep and 3m in diameter and can weigh as much as 1100 kilograms! Imagine it falling on someone!

...Or Not to Nest

But not all birds build nests. The Australian Brush-turkey merely buries its eggs in leaves so that the heat that comes from the decaying vegetation warms them. Birds like auks and murres lay their eggs on bare rocks.

...Or Not Your Own Nest

Cuckoos are really sly and lazy birds. They are known for laying their eggs in another bird's nest, which are incubated by that other bird. And the babies are also reared by them!

Baby Birds

Shell Shocked

A small bird inside an egg has an egg tooth with which it twists and turns the eggshell and makes a big crack along its breadth. As the shell cracks, it pushes hard until it is out, exhausted at the effort.

Bird Bonding

Imprinting is the period in which a bird bonds with its mother and is necessary to learning. When a duck or a chick comes out of its egg, the first thing it sees, it thinks of it as its mother. So it begins to imitate it and learn its ways. Imprinting is very strong in wood ducks. The mother flies down just when her ducklings are about to hatch and calls out to them when they have. They recognize her voice and jump down around 50 feet safely, to their mother. And they do it only because they trust her.

Hunger Pangs

The amount of food a baby bird needs per day is between one half to its full body weight. Its parents work hard all day to feed it this much. A house wren can feed as many as 1,217 times in 15 hours and 45 minutes.

Game Birds

Game birds, as their name suggests, have been hunted for sport. They include birds like pheasants, grouse, partridges and quails.

Grouse Rouse

The grouse has been hunted with great enthusiasm. When a hunter's dogs are near it, it suddenly comes out from its hiding place in the grass as fast as an arrow and with a loud, whirring sound to startle the hunter.

Weather Feather

Ptarmigans or "snow grouse" change the colour of their feathers from a greyish coat in summer to a white coat in winter as protective colouration. They also grow downy feathers on their feet to prevent them from sinking in the snow.

Turkey's Delight

When the wild turkey goes wild with excitement, or just plain emotional, it can change the colour of its bald head to red, pink, white or blue in a matter of seconds. Its talents don't end here. When it gobbles, you can hear it a whole mile away!

Well Done, Boys!

Charming fellows that they are, male crimson horned pheasants get blue horns and a brightly coloured fold of skin under their throat during the mating season. First, they blow up their horns and slip in behind a rock. Then, when a female walks by, they surprise her by showing off their beauty by dancing and bowing with their wings spread. They sure know how to impress a girl, don't they?

As Proud as a Peacock

The peacock, who is also a pheasant, is not to be left behind. While trying to win over a mate, the male peacock spreads his shimmering tail like a fan and shakes it. Apart from impressing females (called peahens) who don't have these grand tails, the tails also help them ward off predators. When one of them approaches a peacock, it simply lifts up its feathers. This makes it appear as if a lot of eyes are glaring back at the enemy who then runs away, scared.

Birds of Prey

Also called raptors, meaning "to seize and carry off" in Latin, birds of prey include hawks, eagles, vultures, falcons, secretary birds and owls. They have hooked beaks and sharp claws called talons to easily grasp, carry and kill their prey. All of them kill live animals or feed upon dead ones.

Most of these birds tend to be quite large and strong, with good eyesight but little or no sense of smell. In most species, female birds are larger than the male ones.

Birdy Long Legs

Known for killing snakes, the secretary bird is different from almost all the birds of prey because it mainly stays and hunts on the ground. Since it has long legs and is very agile, it can safely strike its prey from a safe distance. And if the prey still doesn't die, it flies and drops it from a height.

But what if the snake bites its legs? Well, it has thick scales on them to protect it from snakebites.

Scavenger Squad

Vultures feed on dead and decaying animals. Unlike eagles, vultures don't have hooked and sharp talons, so they aren't equipped for killing. To make their duty of cleaning up more convenient, nature has done a little make up for them—they have no feathers from the neck upwards. Thus, the decaying objects don't get stuck in the feathers and cause bacteria to grow while eating. Flaunting their outstanding flying skills, they soar for hours without flapping wings. Isn't that just impressive?

Hawks vs Eagles

Hawks are often mistaken for eagles. But they are usually smaller than eagles and attack more swiftly.

Eagle Power

Eagles were the symbol of power in ancient Rome and the bald eagle is the national symbol of the United States of America. But apart from hunting its own prey, it also steals what other animals have killed and feeds on carrion. That is why Benjamin Franklin didn't want it to become the national symbol.

Size Doesn't Matter

The golden eagle is so fierce that it can even attack a fully grown deer!

Heavyweight Flyer

The Andean condor is one of the largest flying birds and can weigh up to 15 kg. To bear its weight, their wingspans can be as long as 10.5 feet!

Bird Features: Owls

The owl is a nocturnal bird of prey, that is, it is active at night. It has sharp eyesight and a keen sense of hearing.

Wise Owls

Owls have been associated with intelligence because they signalled future events. The owl was thus the bird of Athena, the Greek goddess of practical wisdom. And because of their nocturnal nature and their haunting sounds, they were also objects of fear and superstition.

Looking Back

Owls can rotate their heads more than 180 degrees both to their right and to their left. So you can actually see an owl with its head backwards and its body to the front. Good heavens!

The Owl and the Skunk

The foul smelling spray of the skunk is useless against the great horned owl because it cannot smell. And that is why this is the owl's favourite food!

Smooth Flight

The feathers of an owl are soft, so that it flies so quietly that its prey can't hear it.

Barn Owls

The most commonly found owls, Barn Owls are found everywhere except in deserts and Polar Regions. They have an uncommon sense of hearing that not only allows them to hunt at night but also to pick up prey from beneath snow or soil.

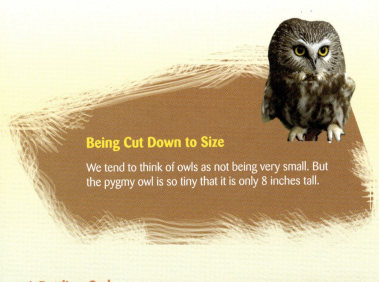

Being Cut Down to Size

We tend to think of owls as not being very small. But the pygmy owl is so tiny that it is only 8 inches tall.

A Rattling Owl

The burrowing owl protects itself by imitating the rattling sound of a rattlesnake when a predator peeps into its underground home.

Songbirds

Songbirds are known so not because they all sing well (a lot of them do) or even sing, but because their vocal organs are highly developed. Some of the well known ones are blackbirds, sparrows, canaries, crows, swallows, robins and thrushes.

A songbird has a song box in its chest and we hear it singing when it passes air through it. It sings for two main reasons: to defend its territory and for courtship.

A Sweeping Majority

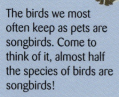

The birds we most often keep as pets are songbirds. Come to think of it, almost half the species of birds are songbirds!

Singathon

A male Carolina wren in captivity is said to have sung around 3,000 times in a single day.

An Illustrious Family

The family most known for its singing skills is the thrush family which includes robins, nightingales, bluebirds and of course, those we call thrushes.

The European nightingale can sing melodious songs in chords of different notes at the same time. When the robin, also a thrush and often seen in parks in North America, warbles cheerily, cheer up, cheerily, cheerily, we know that its springtime!

A Cardinal Sin

While defending their territory, males can show aggression and often attack other males who dare to barge in. And that is why, cardinals sometimes bang against glass windows, thinking that their own reflection is an intruder.

No Greater Love

A lot of times, bluebirds lay their eggs twice in a season. And sometimes, elder siblings among bluebirds stay back to care for the next batch of young bluebirds.

Brainy Crows

To be sure, even crows are songbirds, even with the short and harsh "caws" that most of them have. But that doesn't stop members of the crow family, which includes magpies and ravens, from being the smartest of the lot. Of all the birds, they have the largest brains with the most number of brain cells.

A Barking Bird

A mockingbird can imitate a dog's bark and a hen's cackle. It can also imitate a wide variety of the sounds of other birds. The common mockingbird can mimic the songs of 39 birds apart from its own beautiful voice.

Flightless birds

There was a time, millions of years ago when all birds could fly. But as time passed, they lost their ability to fly.

Scientists think that this happened because these birds lived in islands or places that were separate from others. So they faced no predators and did not need to fly to escape them. As they evolved, they stopped flying altogether.

A Very Talented Bird

The Ostriches of Africa are not only the largest flightless birds but also the largest living birds. An adult male can grow taller than 3m. But that's not all. To escape its enemies, it can run at speeds as high as 75 km per hour and if cornered, can kick very hard. It also lays the largest egg in the world which weighs around 1.4 kg and is 15 cm long and 12 cm wide. Surely, the ostrich deserves an applause!

Why Does the Ostrich Bury Its Head in the Sand?

When in danger, it tries to hide by lying on the ground with its neck stretched out. So it looks as if it is burying its head in the sand.

Changing Direction

Although their large wings can't be used by the Greater Rhea to fly, they use them to alter direction and balance themselves while they're on the run from predators. Their long and powerful legs add the necessary speed to escape quickly.

Sleek Swimmers

Penguins are swimming champions but cannot fly—the only birds to do so. They live only in the Southern Hemisphere. Like dolphins, they leap gracefully from the water (as high as 2m) to take a breath of air. Even though they live on land, they don't know how to eat anything from there and only eat seafood.

To look for food, an adult gentoo penguin can dive into the water 450 times a day!

A Loving Father

Unlike many other birds, male emperor penguins do not sit on their eggs and chicks. They balance them on their feet to protect and cover them with feathered skin called a brood pouch. While the female is away for two months, the males eat absolutely nothing in the cold Antarctic weather and lose a third of their body weight.

An Extinct Flightless Bird: The Dodo

The dodo was a flightless bird in the island of Mauritius in the Indian Ocean. It had a big head, blue-grey feathers, heavy legs which were yellow and a dark bill with a reddish hooked tip. When the Portuguese arrived here in 1507, sailors hunted them in large numbers and killed them with clubs. Rats and pigs, brought to the island by European settlers ate its eggs, which were laid on the ground. By 1690, all dodos were extinct; it was the first bird to be extinct in the modern period.

Waterfowl

Swan Lake

Swans' legs are towards the back of the body which gives them more power while paddling in water. This is also why they look clumsy while walking. And since they have heavy bodies, they run on water for a distance like planes before takeoff.

A male swan is called a cob, a female is known as a pen, while a baby swan is known as a cygnet.

Consisting of ducks, geese, and swans, waterfowls have bigger bodies, shorter legs and webbed feet with bills that tend to be flat.

Geese Save Rome

Geese, like other birds hear much better than us humans. In ancient Rome, when the Goths attacked at night, geese heard them and started honking loudly. This alerted the army who successfully defended the city.

Why Do Geese Fly in a V-formation?

Imagine a goose flying alone. The air in front pushes against it, making it harder to go forward. But if another goose flies behind it, it doesn't have to face the air that much, since the one before has already cut through the air. So the leader stays in front to save energy for the rest. And to save further energy, the leadership is rotated.

Ducks

Types of Ducks

There are two types of ducks: dabbling ducks and diving ducks. Dabbling ducks live in shallow water and feed without completely going underwater. But they do 'tip over' in the water with their backs in the air to get food. Mallards are the most common dappling ducks. On the other hand, diving ducks can dive deep inside. They are therefore heavier (this helps them sink) and find it more difficult to fly.

Either Eider

Soft down feathers which line the nests of eider ducks are used to fill pillows and quilts. There is even a type of quilt named after it—the eiderdown.

A Ducky Thing

A study done by psychologist (one who studies human and animal behaviour) Richard Wiseman and his colleagues in 2002 showed that of all animals, we find ducks the most funny and the most silly. If you have to tell a joke about any animal try one about a duck!

Quack No More

We tend to think that all ducks 'quack'. But the truth is that only the females of most dabbling ducks do so. As for the rest, they whistle, coo, yodel and grunt but they don't quack. A diving duck called scaup makes a noise which goes 'sqaup' and that's how it gets its name.

Parrots

Bright colours, wit, intelligence and last but not the least—imitating humans. This is how parrots, a family that consists of more than 350 species, are known and loved by us.

Best Foot Forward

Parrots use their feet like we use our hands—for climbing and holding food and things. The similarity doesn't end there. There are left and right footed parrots, just the way we are left or right handed!

Puffy Parrots

The red-fan parrot has slightly long feathers in its neck which it can raise when it wants to turn it into a fan. It does this to make itself look larger than it already is, to scare its enemy off.

Happy Eating Clay

In the Amazon basin, you can find parrots and macaws eating clay. They don't really do this to fill their tummies, but to remove the effect of poisons or harmful things in the food they've eaten.

Loves of a Bird

Lovebirds marry for life and can be seen sitting side by side for a long time and preening each other. They're so loving that they snuggle and preen even their favourite human beings!

Word Builder

Budgerigars are one of the five best talkers amongst parrots. When a budgerigar named Sparkie Williams who won a talking contest in England died, he knew 531 words and 383 sentences!

Gift of the Gab

Male African Grey Parrots are the smoothest talkers amongst parrots. Not only can they imitate other birds, but they can also connect words with their meanings, apply our ideas of shape, colour, number etc. An African Grey named Alex could reply to questions such as "How many red squares?" and could do many things chimpanzees, dolphins and even human infants can do. Another one called N'kisi could use words in the correct tense in context and knew around a thousand words.

Attention Seekers

Cockatoos can dance. Conures can lie on their backs when in your hands. Cockatiels will let out a whistle when you pass by. And all this because? Well, to get attention. If you don't give it, be prepared for a tantrum!

Wading Birds

A wading bird is a bird with long legs which goes to shallow water, usually looking for food.

Storks

People in some parts of Europe believe that the stork brings good luck so they make platforms and put baskets to invite storks to nest there. The birth of a child also means that they have been visited by a stork.

Weird Bird

With spoon-like bills that move strangely from side to side, spoonbills wait in shallow water for fish to come by. The moment a fish touches the beak, the spoonbill snaps it shut. And even the noise it makes while eating is slightly weird.

The Pink of Health

After flamingos dip their bill in water, they sway their head while mud is filtered out through small comb-like filters in it. At the same time, the food that they need stays back. They get their pink colour by eating shrimps or plankton. In captivity, they lose their colour if these are not in their diet.

A Moral

Many great blue herons have choked to death by biting more than they could chew. Alas, the fish turned out to be too big for their slender S-shaped necks.

How to spot the difference between a crane and a heron

Cranes	Herons
They have compact feathers that look smooth, growing close to their body.	They have long feathers that look more fluffy.
The back toe of a crane is higher than the toes in front.	A heron's toes don't have any such difference.
The neck is stretched forward while flying and is straight in front.	The neck is folded and pulled back near the body.

Gentleman Cranes

Cranes are well known to take a step and bow in the classic dignified way while courting.

Grey Crowned Crane

Sea Birds

Seabirds are those birds that have adjusted to living a life above and around the sea.

Wings Ahoy!

Albatrosses have enormous wingspans with which they ride the winds and can glide for hours at a stretch without flapping their wings. The wandering albatross has wings that extend for more than 3m! This makes it the greatest wingspan among all birds.

Captain Jack Skua

If you are a bird that might be carrying a fish or some other food back to your nest, you might be attacked by the Arctic Skua who would want to steal it. And that is why they are also known as avian pirates! Beware!

Feeding Gulls

The big herring gull follows ships and fishing boats to feed on garbage that has been thrown from them. It also drops clams from a height onto rocks so that they break and what's inside can be eaten.

Booby Trapped

Boobies got their name from the Spanish word "bobo" which means "dunce" because they seemed clumsy and would foolishly make themselves easy prey. They liked landing on ships where they would be captured and then eaten. Poor boobies!

Dancing Blues

The blue footed booby shows off its blue feet to females and dances with high steps to impress them. Then it looks up to the sky and whistles to complete the show.

Peculiar Pelicans

Pelicans scoop up fish with their stretchable throat pouches. After draining their pouch, they swallow them, satisfied. Great White Pelicans have been known to swallow even other birds like cormorants, gulls, terns and even penguins.

Blooming Beaks

During winter months, the beaks of Atlantic Puffins become dull and grey but they bloom in spring and regain their colour so that they can now attract mates!

Birds and Us

Pigeon Mail

Homing pigeons not only know how to find their home from a place 966 km away, but can also carry our messages at speeds as fast as 72-80 km per hour. The first ones to discover and breed them were the Ancient Egyptians. They have delivered important messages such as Caesar's conquest of Gaul and Napoleon's defeat at Waterloo. Nowadays, the French army still uses them in case normal ways to communicate are not enough and even hospitals use them to send blood and tissue samples faster.

In-Built Radars

Pigeons have a metal called magnetite in their brains which acts as a radar to detect the Earth's magnetic field. The receiver's place is already marked by the pigeon as its home, to which the sender sends it back.

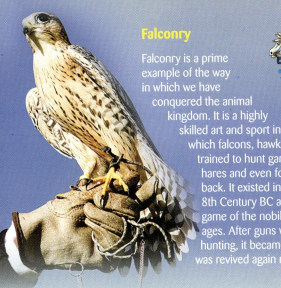

Falconry

Falconry is a prime example of the way in which we have conquered the animal kingdom. It is a highly skilled art and sport in which falcons, hawks and eagles are trained to hunt game like other birds, hares and even foxes and bring them back. It existed in Asia as early as the 8th Century BC and was a favourite game of the nobility in the middle ages. After guns were used for hunting, it became less popular but was revived again recently.

Chicken Feeds

Birds like chickens, duck and geese, which have been domesticated for their meat and eggs are called poultry and are our largest sources of proteins. We consume them so much that in 2003 alone, 76 million tons (1 ton is around 1000 kg) of poultry and 61 million tons of eggs were produced all over the world!

Can You Please Help Me, Honey?

HOWDY MY FOLLOWERS!

The Boran people of East Africa use honeyguides, one of the few birds that like eating beeswax, to assist them in their search for honey and make it quicker. They sound a loud whistle called the "Fuulido" before a honey search which doubles their chances of meeting honeyguides.

Saving the Whooping Crane

Damage to their habitats made the whooping crane almost die out. But efforts at conservation has made numbers of the whooping crane rise gradually from when there were only 18 of them left in 1939. Captive breeding, education of hunters by telling them not to shoot large white birds and the forbidding of aircraft to fly lower than 2000 feet where these birds nest have created a modern example of what we can do to protect birds.

Mammals

They rule the earth. And they can be found from the hottest of places to the coldest. They breathe air, have a backbone and have hair. They also are the most caring when it comes to their babies and feed them milk.

Climate Control

Mammals are warm-blooded or endothermic. Which means that unlike fish, amphibians and reptiles who are cold-blooded or exothermic, the temperature of their bodies does not depend upon whether it's freezing or boiling outside. So, they can be active for a longer time and survive in places which are colder and hotter.

Cold Creature

The Weddell Seal is the closest any mammal comes to the South Pole in Antarctica, living in the coldest weather possible. It carves holes in the ice with the edges of its teeth and dives into the water underneath to find food and to protect itself from storms. Its fur and a thick layer of fat beneath stops heat escaping from its body.

A Fuzzy Feeling

At some time in their lives, all mammals have hair made of keratin. Hair keeps them warm and helps them to blend with their surroundings (called camouflage) to hide. Thicker coats of fur also protect them. Many whales have hair only when they're in the womb. Porcupines have hair that has been turned into sharp spines and cats have whiskers which are sensitive to anything touching them.

Birth Rites

You do have weird mammals like the platypus and the spiny anteater who lay eggs, but as for the rest of the them, they give birth to live young.

Baby Care

Only mammals have mammary glands with which they give nourishment to their infants. That's why the words 'mammal' and 'mammary' are connected.

Brain Waves

The most intelligent of all animals are mammals.
With a complex and highly developed brain, they have an excellent memory and strong powers of learning. This allows them to learn from those with more experience and helps them cope in difficult environments.

Award Winners

And now for the tiny one

Weighing only around 2 grams and 2.7 to 3.3 cm in length, the Kitti's Hog-Nosed Bat is the smallest mammal that exists.

And then for the humongous one

Not only is it the largest mammal, the blue whale is also the largest animal ever. As long as 100 feet and weighing more than 1,81,000 kg, its tongue is as heavy as an elephant and its heart as bulky as a car.

Primates

With hands that grasp, eyes that look forward and brains that are large, primates are the smartest of all the mammals. There are two types of them: the lower primates which include lemurs, lorises and tarsiers and the higher primates which comprise monkeys, apes and humans.

From Chimp to Champ

You can see how chimpanzees are related to us when you see them using tools. They can make and use tools to pick out insects and grubs from their nests and logs. You can watch them smashing open a nut with a stone and using a leaf as a sponge to soak water to drink. They also have the brains to use some basic human sign language. Indeed, we did descend from a common ancestor who lived around four to eight million years ago.

Gentle Does It

In fiction, we often encounter gorillas as vicious and ferocious. But in reality, they're really the most peaceful of all apes and are almost completely vegetarian. And yes, they're the largest primates and can be as heavy as 270 kg.

Baboon Bonding

Baboons like the safety and security of large groups called troops led by one ruling male. The hamadryas baboons form large troops up to a thousand and bond the same way other monkeys do. They groom each other by stroking and combing another's fur. That way, they keep each other happy.

Slim Superheroes

Using their tails as their fifth arm to pick objects with and hold branches, spider monkeys look like spiders in the highest reaches of rainforests. Obviously, that's how they get their name.

Lemur Lore

Madagascar is a unique island the only place where lemurs can be found. The sifaka, a type of lemur, can leap as far as 10 meters with its body straight from one branch to another.

Aye-Aye Captain!

Acute hearing and a strange-looking middle finger that looks like a twig combine to help the aye-aye, another lemur, find prey that no other mammal can get to. It taps its fingers eight times a second to look for hollows in the trunk of a tree where beetle grubs might lie. On finding them, it gnaws through the wood and digs them out with its twig finger.

The Cat Family

Although ruthless when it comes to their prey, members of the cat family are generally lonely creatures. The most carnivorous of all meat eaters, they are excellent hunters with night vision, claws that can be hidden and sharp canine teeth. They silently stalk their victims and then pounce upon them in a surprise attack. So, they're called ambush predators.

Cat Got Your Tongue?

Not only domestic cats, but all cats purr when they're satisfied. They have really rough tongues with which they clean themselves.

A Long Catnap

It was the Egyptians who, 5000 years ago, mastered the domestication of cats. Apart from helping them get rid of rats and mice, cats also helped them to hunt birds and fish. In return, Egyptians worshipped them, mummified them so they can live with their master in the afterlife and buried them in a special cemetery. One of them was found to have more than 300,000 preserved cats!

A Lion's Pride

Known as the "king of the beasts," lions stand for strength and majesty. Of all the cats, they're unique in that they live in a group, called a pride. They protect it with great ferocity, roaming large territories which usually covers an area of 260 square kilometres. So strong is their bite that they can kill a zebra by lodging their canines in its neck.

Tiger Trouble

Found only in Asia and mostly in India, tigers are very slithery predators. Their stripes merge with the grass and forest around them, making them almost invisible. Their soft paws make them silent, and they move only when the prey is not looking. They even kill humans sometimes, but only if there's shortage of prey, in self-defence , if they're weak, old or if it's a tigress with cubs. There was a tiger that is said to have killed 127 people in a single year!

Follow the Cheetah

From 0 to 96 kilometres an hour in only 3 seconds. No, this isn't a fast car, but the fastest land animal – the cheetah. With its fastest recorded sprint being at 114 km per hour, it usually goes at 80-100 km per hour while chasing its prey. Even at those speeds, it can make rapid and sudden turns to get to them.

Getting a Grip

Sharp claws and large paws allow the clouded leopard to hang upside down on branches large and strong enough to support them.

Going Up?

A puma might not be able to roar and its call is a louder version of the domestic cat's, but it sure can leap as high as 5m from the ground!

Dog Days

From the cold Arctic where Arctic Foxes live, to fennecs in the blazing Sahara Desert, members of the dog family or canines as they are called, are found everywhere in the world. They're on the slender side and have long muzzles, long legs, and bushy tails. And yes, they are famous for their sense of smell and keen hearing, the sense of smell being a million times stronger than ours.

It's a Dog's Life

It is highly likely that man's best friends were the first animals to be domesticated. Their relationship to their wild cousins can still be seen when they dig up the garden to hide bones or their loved toy to preserve it for later, just like the wild ones bury meat to save it up for a future meal. Also, they mark their territories by urinating on posts, trees and the like so the scent can tell other dogs to keep away and they ward off intruders the way those in the wild do.

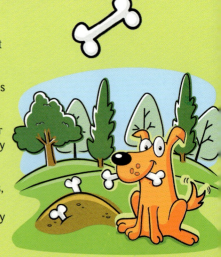

The Legacy of Dogs

Every year, the Iditarod Trail Sled Dog Race is run for a distance of around 1770 km between Anchorage and Nome in Alaska.

A test of endurance and courage, each sled is pulled by 12 to 16 dogs who are handled by a person called a musher. One of the reasons why it is run is to remember how teams of dogs travelled hundreds of miles with medicines in 1925 to Nome so that children could be saved from diphtheria, a fatal disease.

Hunting Beasts

Having only four toes rather than five which the rest of the dogs have, African hunting dogs who hunt in packs of 15 to 60 also distinguish themselves by being able to overpower and eat prey ten times their size.

Wolf Wolf!

Wolves, like other dogs are highly social, and hunt in packs of six to ten, and can travel 20 km in a single day. They rule according to rank, with the senior most being a male wolf and his mate. Only they are allowed to reproduce and are called the alpha pair. The rest in the pack take care of their pups.

Wild, Wild West

Coyotes are known for their mournful howls to warn rivals to keep away. Found in the western North America, the picture of them with the outlines of their heads raised against the moon symbolized the Wild West.

Foxy Fashions

We humans aren't the only ones who change fashions. Come winter, Arctic Foxes change the colour of their fur from brown to white. While in summer, they blend themselves with meadows, in winters, they match with the snow as a form of camouflage. The short timings of days in winter give rise to hormones which enable them to transform in this way.

Rodents and Rabbits

We don't like rats and mice in our houses, but we find some other rodents, adorable. We like keeping rabbits as pets. What makes rodents and rabbits different from other mammals are their upper and lower teeth (incisors) which grow throughout their lives.

They nibble and gnaw a lot at hard objects. This is not only to sharpen their incisors, but also because if they don't, they'll either not be able to eat or they'll grow into the skull, leading to their death.

What's the difference between a hare and a rabbit?

Hares are slightly larger than rabbits, with longer hind legs and ears.	Rabbits have burrows in which they raise their children and hares just conceal them on the ground.
Hares can also run faster and can reach up to 72 km per hour.	A baby hare is called a leveret. Whereas a baby rabbit is often called a kitten.

Great Expectations

We might think that rodents are really small, but the capybara of South and Central America grows up to half the size of a fully grown pig 1.2m in length and weighing 50 kg!

Chipmunks

Adorable! Well, that goes for chipmunks. They have pouches in their cheeks which they fill with nuts and seeds and carry them to their burrows. In winter, they don't use up their body fat but use the food they have gathered to keep themselves going.

Prairie Dog

Prairie dogs kiss or nuzzle while greeting each other in their long-winded underground burrows, full of tunnels and chambers. They even have nurseries, bedrooms and toilets. The black-tailed prairie dog lives in huge communities called towns. Such a town was found that covered an area of 65,000 square km in Texas with 400 million members!

Brother Beaver

Beavers really work hard to build their homes. They build a dam by making a foundation with thousands of logs and sticks. Then they add more of these and stones and mud till the barrier is strong and watertight and up to 90m high. Next to the dam, they build their house, which is called a lodge, made out of criss-crossing branches plastered with dead leaves and clay. This is covered by a roof. What's more, lodges have underwater tunnels which are the entrances, making them safe from predators.

Hoofed Animals

Hoofed animals actually tiptoe all the time and their tough and insensitive hooves allow them to do that. The heels of their feet were like ours a long time ago. Gradually over the years their nails turned into hooves.

There are two main groups of hoofed animals. Odd-toed animals like horses and rhinos where one central toe bears most of the weight. And even-toed animals like camels where both toes carry their weight.

Why Do Cows Chew Cud?

The grass and other plants which they eat are a bit hard to digest. So they first swallow the grass which softens in the first chamber of the stomach, called the rumen (that's why this class is called ruminants). This grass, called cud is partly digested and goes back to the mouth, chewed again and then finally digested.

Duel for Honour

If a hoofed animal has horns or antlers, then it's safe when it fights. When they fight, they just lock their antlers and push them (called sparring). Then they come to recognise who's stronger and the struggle ends there.

Striped Stores

No two zebras have the same stripes, just like our fingerprints. They might be there so they can recognise each other and make stronger bonds. Or to confuse predators so that they only see a blaze of passing stripes and can't single out a zebra in a running herd. But zebras aren't really that united. Males fight against each other with bites and kicks to win their wives to the point that one of them even dies sometimes.

Bears

A lovable and cuddly bear? Or a wild and vicious one? Actually most bears are neither and are violent only if they're low on food or if their cubs are threatened. They're powerful, as smart as dogs and can stand on their hind legs like us!

Grizzly Talent

Like Winnie the Pooh, grizzly bears love their honey. But they're also fierce and strong enough to carry off small horses and cattle. In cold Alaska, they keep their mouths open in water to wait for salmon to hop in and can eat 40 kg of fish a day. They are mammals who can survive the longest without food all of six months. Thanks to the fat they've stored from the sweet things they've eaten. They can find these goodies because they've got a map of where to get each of them in their heads.

Running Along

They might be huge and look clumsy while walking, but don't be deceived. Brown bears can run as fast as 48 km per hour! You can't win a race with them, can you?

To Bear or not to Bear?

Polar bears have to deal with the cold and the cubs face the risk of being killed by adult males. Luckily, they've got their ways. For the cold, they have transparent fur which allows sunlight to pass through so that heat can get absorbed by their black skin, under which is a layer of fat which also helps. As for the cubs, their mother defends and protects them fiercely, so they're in good hands.

Look! No teeth.

It can't see or hear well, but a sloth bear can sure smell its way through. Roaming mostly in the night, it digs and rips out colonies of bees or termites with its large front paws, puts its long snout, closes its nostrils and sucks them. And the sucking is all the better because it lacks front upper teeth!

A Longish Tongue

It was thought that the golden or white crescent on the chest of the Malayan Sun Bear stood for the rising sun. But the insects it feeds on might see its tongue as the shadow of the rising sun, since its really long tongue reaches them deep inside their hiding places. Also to lick honey with!

Bear Watching

A spectacled bear has white or yellowish rings around its eyes that look like spectacles. Besides catching mice and birds it especially likes to eat fruits. To eat the juicy fruits it can go to any lengths. So, the spectacled bear, away from his lair blowing puffs of air, just sits and stares on a snug platform on the tree waiting for the fruit to ripen and fall.

The Weasel Family

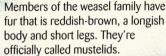

Members of the weasel family have fur that is reddish-brown, a longish body and short legs. They're officially called mustelids.

Never out of Step

A weasel war dance is often done by weasels and ferrets. They hop sideways and backwards with their tails all frizzy, backs arched and with lots of hissing. Ferrets can clumsily bump into things and stumble over objects while they do this. It is thought that they do this in the wild to confuse their prey and domestic ones do it after playing or capturing a toy or something they like.

Back Stroke

Sea otters float cooly on their backs in groups when they're sleeping. And they sometimes knot themselves in kelp or seaweed forests so that the sea current doesn't carry them away.

Home Comforts

The stoat is a cunning creature. It doesn't like building its own burrow and lives in burrows and nest chambers of rodents it has killed and lines them with their skin and inner fur. It also lives in log piles, under tree roots, inside rocks and even in the nests of magpies.

I'm Digging It!

Badgers are well known for their digging skills appreciated by coyotes too. So American Badgers and coyotes form a partnership to hunt prey efficiently leaving them little space to escape. When a prey like a squirrel dodges the coyote by going into its burrow, the badger digs it up. And whenever it runs away from the badger, the swift coyote catches it.

Skunk

Last but not the least, the skunk should be mentioned for the famous way in which it annoys its predator. It turns around and sprays a terrible smelling liquid, a blast which can reach 3m. And this is one tough stink to get rid of for the predator.

Large Land Mammals

Elephant News

Elephants are the largest animals that walk on land. Weighing up to 8000 kg and as high as 3 to 4m from the shoulder, the African Savanna elephant is the largest elephant. The Asian elephant is different. It is smaller and averages 2.7m, has two fingers rather than one on the trunk, and its ears are smaller and rounder.

Trunk Shakes

Elephants can be found greeting each other either by touching the other's face or by interlocking their trunks. This acts like our own handshake!

Elephants, giraffes, hippos and rhinos are protected from predators by their sheer size. Who wouldn't think twice before attacking? They are the giants who roam the earth and we're proud to have them with us!

Happy Hippos

Hippos spend as much as 16 hours a day in water so they can keep cool in the hot African weather and also because water supports their weight. There was a myth that they sweated blood, but that's just the natural sunblock lotion and skin moisturizer that they secrete.

Indian Armoured Forces

Indian rhinos have only one horn and a thick hide with flexible skin in between for movement. These features make them different from other rhinos. The hide looks and acts like an armour and protects it. And though it might weigh around 2000 kg, it can sprint at speeds as fast as 48 km per hour!

Marsupials

Marsupials are well known for carrying their babies in a pouch called a 'marsupium'. When their babies are born, they're really tiny and underdeveloped. Then they make a difficult journey to the pouch where they attach themselves to the mother's nipples and are taken care of there.

The Kick Boxer

When a kangaroo is born (called a 'joey'), it is only about 2.5 cm long and weighs less than a gram. But when it grows up, a male grey kangaroo can grow up to 2.1m and have very powerful hind legs with which they can jump as far as 10m and 1.8m high. And it can box another male for female mates by leaning back on its tail and kicking hard with the hind legs.

Can't Bear It Anymore

Actually, koala 'bears' aren't bears at all but marsupials. We call them that because they look like our own toy teddy bears. They feed on eucalyptus leaves which are quite poor on nutrients. So to make up for the lack of energy, they sleep every day for as long as 18 hours.

Playing Possum

Either opossums are trying to be funny, or they're clever. When a predator attacks them, they flop to one side, lie still and close their eyes or stare like a dead person. The best bit is when they stick their tongues out, completing the act to perfection. The predator is now surprised that it's dead and then the opossum escapes.

Mamma's Boy

Even after they've come out of their mother's pouch in which they've been for five months, young wombats still return to the pouch to get away from danger or to nurse. By seven months, they are more independent.

Crazy Devil

Just like in cartoons, the Tasmanian devil is as crazy as can be. When the largest marsupial carnivore loses its temper, it bares its teeth, lunges, and growls that are quite scary. It's not surprising that early European settlers called it a "devil". Its strong jaws used to crush bones make it look more like one.

Mammals in Water

Around 50 million years ago, a lot of mammals decided to leave land for water. As time passed, their forelimbs became flippers and their bodies became more streamlined to swim.

What's your porpoise?

Porpoises are confused for dolphins and are closely related. The difference is that dolphins have a beak-like snout and conical teeth whereas porpoises don't and have flat teeth.

Both are really intelligent and have a complex system of communication with high pitched whistles and squeaks. They also send a sound to an object and when it bounces off and returns, they can judge. This they do by understanding how much time it took for the echo.

Trick and Treat

Many complex tricks can be taught to dolphins. Bottlenose dolphins have been seen to jump till heights of 4m above water and land back with a splash on their back or side. Watching these playful mammals is certainly a treat!

Helping Hands

Dolphins are very social. They hunt in huge groups called pods to trap fish. They help injured dolphins and take them to the surface to breathe.

Sea Unicorns

Since the narwhal has tusks like a unicorn's, traders in the past used to pass them off as unicorn's horns and sold them for lots of gold. People bought them because they thought that cups made of unicorns' horns will remove the poison from any drink poured in them.

Deadly Playmates

Deadly predators who even hunt whales, killer whales or orca can jump from the sea and snap a seal right from the ice. Although since they're dolphins, they too can be trained by us.

A Whale of a Time

Known for songs that travel miles across the ocean, humpback whales can compose songs that last for 5-35 minutes. They migrate all the way from the polar parts of the sea in summer to warm tropical waters in winter, a distance of around 25,000 km, to only give birth and mate. Many males race and fight to win their ladylove.

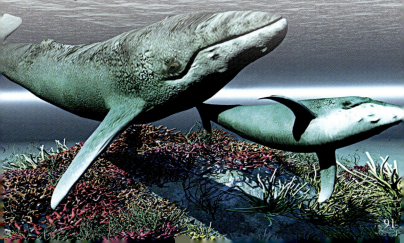

Larger than Life

It's not just their huge size that matters. Blue whales not only spray water up to heights of 9m in the air from their blowholes but also eat about 3600 kg of krill (a small creature like a shrimp) everyday.

Saving Up

Seals, sea lions and walruses, also called pinnipeds, reduce their pulse rate while diving so they can save up on oxygen. But in the end, they have to return to land and that's how they differ from whales.

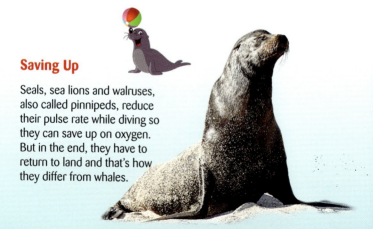

Armed to the Teeth

Walruses use their tusks to show off to females and the one with the longest tusks gets to be the leader of a group!

Mercows

Called sea cows because of the slow speed at which they move and the sea grass they graze on, dugongs and manatees can be mistaken for a swimming person. That is why a lot of people think that this has led to the stories and myths about mermaids.

Bats

Sound Bites

Like dolphins and a few other mammals, bats find their way in the dark by sending out high-pitched cries in which they click 200 times a second. When this bounces off objects, bats hear these echoes to form pictures and judge their direction, distance, speed and size. This process is called echolocation. And on a dark night in a thick forest, on their way to catching their prey, they don't bump into anything at all!

Although a few mammals can glide, bats are the only ones who can actually fly by flapping their wings. Unlike birds who have feathers, bats have wings which are covered with skin joined to their fingers.

Nosey Parkers

Bats have funny-looking outgrowths on their noses to let out their sounds and focus their calls .Those on the nose of horseshoe bats look like leaves or horseshoes.

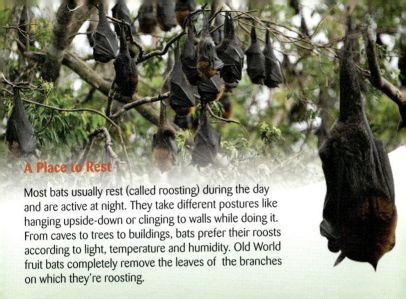

A Place to Rest

Most bats usually rest (called roosting) during the day and are active at night. They take different postures like hanging upside-down or clinging to walls while doing it. From caves to trees to buildings, bats prefer their roosts according to light, temperature and humidity. Old World fruit bats completely remove the leaves of the branches on which they're roosting.

Blood Suckers

Yes, vampire bats have inspired our stories about blood-sucking vampires. And blood is all they drink. Found in Mexico, Central and South America, they mostly feed on cattle and horses, but they've also fed on humans. A colony of 100 of them can drink the blood of 25 cows in a single year!

Odd Ones Out

Mammals are of three kinds: placental, marsupial and monotremes. Placental mammals are those who nourish their children through a structure called placenta and marsupials are those who shelter and feed them in a pouch. The odd ones out are monotremes who lay eggs. And there are only two of them the duck-billed platypus and the echidna or spiny anteater.

Sweet Poison

When some stuffed duck-billed platypuses were sent to England from Australia, scientists thought it was a prank in which duck bills were sewn to a mammal's body. But when live ones were sent, they realized that they were real. Platypuses have 'bills' and webbed feet like a duck's, tails like a beavers and a long slender body of an otter's. And though we may think that they look sweet, they have poisonous stingers on their heels!

All Mixed Up

Echidnas have long, sticky tongues to eat ants like an anteater's and bodies with spikes like hedgehogs and porcupines. But not only are they different from them, they also carry their eggs in pouches unlike platypuses, who lay them in nests.

Other Oddities
Tigons and Ligers

If a male lion and a female tiger mate, the offspring is a mixed-breed called a liger. And if a lioness and a male tiger mate, it's called a tigon. The breeding is only done in zoos and tigons and ligers are larger and darker than their parents. They can't have children, except for females who sometimes do.

Downside Up

Instead of going down, the babirusa's tusks grow upwards. And out of all things in the world, they try to catch attention with these peculiar things.

Migration

Migrations are seasonal movements when animals travel in search of food, a different habitat or climate.

Through Land and Snow

In the North American Arctic tundra , reindeer or Caribou as they are called in North America, make the longest migration of all land mammals in herds that go up till 500,000. They travel a distance of up to 5000 km between cold tundra regions and warmer forest regions every year.

Straw coloured bat

In some parts of Africa in late October, you'll find the sky swarming with huge groups of African straw-coloured bats, with up to hundreds of thousands above you. And if you find yourself in the swamps of Kasanka National Park in Zambia, you will find about ten million of these, who have come from all over Central Africa to feed on mangoes and other fruits. This is also where you'll find at the time, the largest roost of bats in the world!

Grey Whale

The longest length to which any mammal goes is the grey whale. Since their calves don't have enough fat (blubber as it is called) to keep them warm in the cold arctic, grey whales have to swim 10,000 km to the subtropical waters of Baja, Mexico to breed during winter. They find their way by following the coastline.

Living Together

Apart from domestic animals, here are a few other ways in which we all share a relationship.

Moosing Around

If you go to the city of Anchorage in Alaska, you might bump into a moose. Or you might find one lazing around in someone's swimming pool. And this is because it has a population of 250 moose in summer and up to 1000 in winter!

Sacred Mammals

In India, animals like cows and the Hanuman langur are considered sacred by Hindus. So you can find cows freely roaming the streets and langurs, who are named after the god Hanuman, in temples.

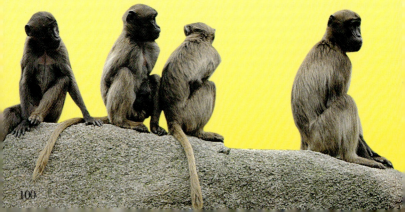

Animal Testing

Scientists use mammals like guinea pigs, hamsters, mice, rabbits, monkeys and apes to conduct research. Mice share 99 per cent of our genes, so they are used to understand how we inherit diseases from our parents. Primates other than humans are used since their brains are similar to ours. The first chimp to be launched into outer space was Ham in 1961 who was trained to push a lever five seconds after he saw a blue light flashing.

The Panda's Plight

Many animals have become extinct or endangered due to hunting by us and destruction of their habitat. Giant pandas almost became extinct (this is when an animal is endangered) because of both reasons. They died of starvation because of the bamboo forests they fed on were destroyed. There might be lesser than 1000 pandas in the wild and around 150 in zoos. Efforts made to preserve them include the Chinese government creating nature reserves for them and lending them to countries as a sign of friendship.

Reptiles

It might not be Halloween. And yet reptiles can look scary. But that's just because all reptiles are covered with dry scales and not hair or feathers (Imagine a feathery reptile!). Also, they breathe air and have a backbone.

Blow Hot, Blow Cold

Reptiles are cold-blooded creatures. That means that if it's hot outside, then the temperature of their bodies will be hot. If it is cold outside, their bodies will be cold. Whereas we mammals are warm-blooded, which means we can control our body temperature.

Basking and Brumation

One can find reptiles sunbathing and they don't do this for a tan, but to keep their bodies warm. This is called basking. If they're cold, they get lazy and aren't able to move quickly then. So, when temperatures drop, reptiles get very lethargic to save energy. This is when they hibernate (called brumation in case of reptiles). But unlike mammals, they don't actually sleep or live off reserves of fat.

We're Really Old

Fossils of reptiles have been found that are more than 300 million years old! They ruled life on land for more than 150 million years and birds and mammals are their descendants.

Turning Over a New Leaf

Reptiles shed their scales and replace them throughout their life. Most of them shed their scales one by one or in patches but snakes shed all of them at one go.

Born with a Tooth

All reptile babies have an egg tooth which sharply juts out from their snouts. This is there so that they can cut through the thick shells of their eggs to come out into the world.

Flippers

Coming Through…

Reptiles have some very interesting ways of finding their way around the world. Snakes and some lizards push the scales of their bellies against the ground to get a grip and then pull their bodies so that they can move forward. Sea turtles swim with the help of flippers or webbed feet and alligators and crocodiles move through water by lashing their tails. And even though no known reptile can fly, there are only a few snakes and lizards that can glide across the air. Fortunately!

Reptile Myths

Dragon Power

Whether fire-breathing or not fire-breathing, the dragons of myth have usually been shown as reptiles—they hatch from eggs and have scaly bodies. Europeans showed dragons with bat-like wings and were mostly considered evil whereas Chinese dragons do look like huge snakes but are forces of good.

The Evil Serpent

In Jewish and Christian traditions, it is held that it was a snake who misled the first humans, Adam and Eve and that is how evil came into the world. And so the snake was cursed to crawl on its belly in shame.

Early Christians disliked the snake so much that there is a famous story in which it is said that St. Patrick drove out all the snakes from Ireland with his staff and that is why there are no snakes in Ireland! Try figuring out the real reason yourself and see what you come up with.

On the Back of the Turtle

A lot of ancient myths thought the turtle to stand for stability. There are legends in places as far apart as India, Japan and North America that the earth was supported on the back of a turtle with nothing else to support it. And one still wonders who might have supported the turtle?

Tuatara

It looks like a lizard but is not actually one. The tuatara is found only on around 32 islands off the coast of New Zealand. They've survived on these islands because there are no rats there who like to eat these reptiles. This is because New Zealand split away from the major landmass a long time back and separated from rats too.

As of now, not even people are allowed on them (if people come, rats will join). Anyway, these islands are surrounded by huge cliffs which makes it tough for ships to land.

A Long Egg-spectation

A tuatara stays in its egg for fifteen months before it hatches. This is the longest any reptile stays in its egg.

If Music be the Food...

These music-lovers can actually come out of their holes to hear someone singing. They like solos but they prefer a rousing chorus and are more likely to come out during that!

Ooh Spikey!

They have sharp and bony spikes along their backs, just like dinosaurs. They've been around for 240 million years and are survivors from the age of dinosaurs and that's why, they're called 'living fossils'.

Meet the Lizards

Six-lined Racerunner

We lizards like living in warm places and are found in places that range from wet tropics to dry deserts.

Speed Demons

Most lizards have strong muscular legs and can travel really fast. The racerunner maybe short and only 20 to 40 cm long, but can run as fast as 24 km per hour. Not only that, the fastest lizard in the world is the Black Spiny-tailed Iguana which grows up to 1.5m for males and 1m for females and can run as fast as 34.9 km per hour!

A Lucky Break

Many species of lizard have tails that break off when touched. These broken tails wriggle even then, which distracts the predator. This lizard now takes advantage of this opportunity to escape. And yes, the tail grows back!

Lizard Profiles

Green Basilisk Lizard

To escape from danger it can run on water without sinking for as long as 4m! After that, being a very good swimmer, it can quickly go underwater and remain there for 30 minutes.

Not only that, this dandy lizard has a high crest on its head and back to charm the ladies.

The Little Webbed Wonder

The webbed feet gecko is at home in the reddish sands of the Namib Desert. Its webbed feet help it glide across the sand quickly and bury itself in it and its colour helps it camouflage itself.

A Gecko's Grip

Geckos can climb the most slippery surfaces, even glass windows! This is because their feet have sticky plates under which are millions of really tiny hairs which help it to cling firmly.

A Brave Coward?

The frilled lizard is quite an amusing creature. When it feels threatened, it opens its mouth, spreads its flaps and hisses fiercely. And yet, if the attacker doesn't go anywhere, the lizard simply does an about turn and flees for dear life.

Take Cover...

Draco lizards have folds which are extensions of their ribs. They take these out, spread them and fly, gliding as far as 10m. This is done to escape predators, find food and to get mates.

Smart Guys

They're fast and quick tongued. Not witty, of course, but they have a tongue that's 50 centimetres long which they flick in the blink of an eye to gobble up their prey.

Scary huh!

The green anole lizard has a throat sac that is enlarged (called a 'dewlap') and brightly coloured. In order to defend its territory, it blows up the dewlap to scare male anoles or other animals away.

A Living 'Dragon'

The largest and heaviest of the lizards, reaching around 3m and more than 136 kilos, Komodo dragons can eat water buffalos and have been known to eat even humans. Their saliva is poisonous because around 50 strains of bacteria live there. Once they've bitten a prey, they can follow it for days till the poison works.

Colour for a Cause

The lizards that are famous because they can change the colour of their skin are known as chameleons.

A lot of people think that chameleons change colour to match their surroundings. But that's not true. They do it to show their reactions and emotions or under the influence of the surrounding light and temperature.

Welcome to Madagascar

Half the species of chameleons in the world live on the island of Madagascar itself! What an island!

A Sticky Customer

The chameleon lies still, waiting for a juicy fly to buzz past it. The moment it appears, it shoots out its tongue, which is long and sticky, and pulls it back to munch on its meal.

What's up, Croc?
Crocodile Facts

We're Survivors

We have survived from the age of dinosaurs and have been around for about 80 million years.

Crocodiles vs Alligators

Crocodiles	Alligators
Have narrow V-shaped snouts.	Have a flatter, wider head, which means that their noses are U-shaped.
A crocodile has a large tooth in its lower jaw which shows when its mouth is closed.	For the alligator, this tooth doesn't show.
Crocodiles are more aggressive	Alligators tend to avoid danger.

Unlikely Cousins

You might think that crocodiles are more closely related to other reptiles, but interestingly, their closest relatives are birds.

Chinese Alligator

There are only two species of alligators in the world- the American alligator and the Chinese alligator. The Chinese alligator is almost extinct.

Stomach this!

A crocodile has a very powerful digestive system. It doesn't have grinding teeth, but it can digest all the shells and bones that it eats because alligators and crocodiles have rocks in their tummies called gastroliths that help in digestion. This is all the more surprising because their stomachs are not bigger than our heads!

Crocablanca...or a Crocodile Romance

In their more romantic moods, male crocodiles hum a low tone that can only be detected by a female crocodile, even if she is miles away. When they're together, the male gently rubs the female's snout and blows bubbles underneath her, which release crocodile perfume.

A Gentle Giant?

The ferocious Nile crocodile, also the second largest crocodile, can eat up to half its body weight. But beneath that hard exterior there perhaps lies a soft heart. It softly rolls its eggs in its mouth to help them to hatch (rather than going snap!).

In another example of its gentleness, it has struck a deal (called a symbiotic relationship) with some birds like the Egyptian Plover. The huge crocodile gets rid of blood sucking leeches by opening its mouth wide and allowing the bird to pick them. And so, the bird too benefits by having its meal in the process.

American Alligator

Around 150 million years old, it is a direct survivor from the age of dinosaurs who became extinct 65 million years ago.

Phew!

They were about to become extinct recently, but measures to ensure their protection have made them recover to a population of more than one million.

The Pot at the End of the Nose

Gharials or gavials have a long snout at the end of which there is a bulbous growth which is called a ghara, the Hindi word for "pot". It is called so since it resembles a pot and is used to attract females and also to blow bubbles during courtship.

And The Prizes Go To…

For the Largest Reptile in the World

The Australian saltwater crocodile for growing as long as 7m. This one is dangerous, because it is also the most likely crocodile to eat human.

For the Smallest Croc

The African dwarf crocodile, for hardly growing longer than 1.5m. Cute croc? Perhaps.

Spectacled Caiman

This is the most common of all crocodilians (that's what the whole group is called which includes crocodiles, alligators, gharials and caimans).
That is because they can adapt to both freshwater and salt water. In winter, they have a special pigment in their skin that turns their colour to a darker shade.

Snakes: A Brief Encounter

Snakes are meat-eating reptiles with bodies that are long and slender, no legs, no eyelids, no external ears and broad scales on their bellies to move forward. They also have the familiar forked tongues that flick forward.

Just Looking Around

Snakes find their way around the world and hunt for prey by using their eyes or they can sense vibrations with their bodies. They can flick their tongues to pick up scents from the air to locate things around them. Pit vipers have pits on their heads to sense heat and boas and pythons have them on their lips.

Try swallowing a pumpkin and you'll appreciate the fact that snakes can swallow things that are up to 20 per cent the size of their bodies. This is because its lower jaw is very flexible because its two halves are not tightly attached and so are the joints in its skull.

Ready? Charge!

Snakes can strike or lunge forward to get hold of their prey very fast. Some swallow small animals immediately, others like pythons grip their prey tightly and coil around them till they suffocate, while others inject venom to make them die or to paralyse them. The good news is that only one third of the total snake population is poisonous and people do not often die from snakebites.

Python

Keeping a Snake as a Pet

A lot of people are interested in snakes as pets. If you want to start, then having a Corn Snake is a good way because you can handle and care for it easily and it is non-poisonous.

Inland Taipan

Which country has the most number of poisonous snakes in the world?

Australia is home to nine out of ten of the world's most poisonous snakes, the most venomous of which is the Inland Taipan which can kill a full grown adult in two minutes.

Record Breakers

- The smallest snakes in the world are the blind snakes which are only around 20 cm long.
- The longest snake in the world is the reticulated python which can reach more than 8m in length, while the heaviest being the giant anaconda.
- The longest poisonous snake is the king cobra which reaches a length of around 5m.

Growing Tales

Snakes grow all their lives, a little at a time. Do you wish you grew all your life?

For Your Eyes Only

The next time you happen to see a snake whose eyes are milky coloured and its body looking dull, you will know that it is about to shed its skin.

The Bluffmaster

The hognose snake, even though it is a non-poisonous snake, knows how to bluff its way out of danger. It'll act as if it is a venomous snake, flatten its head, hiss and strike but not bite. If the attacker calls off its bluff, it'll flip on to its back, writhe and bleed from its mouth and act as if it is dead, making itself unappetising to its predator.

A Rattling Snake

A rattlesnake's 'rattle' is made up of keratin, the same pigment that makes up our skin and nails. A new segment is added to the rest of the segments when it sheds its skin. When these segments vibrate against each other, the rattling sound is heard.

King Cobras

- King Cobras can be 5m long—the longest of all poisonous snakes.

- When attacked they can raise one third of their bodies and still thrust forward to attack.

- They are the only snakes that build nests for their eggs and they guard it till their babies hatch.

- The ideal snakes for snake charmers. Although they can hear, they can't hear sounds in their immediate surroundings. And they sway to the shape and the way the flute moves, rather than to its sound.

- The poison in a single bite can kill 20 people or an elephant! But don't worry, they like keeping to themselves and are only hostile if someone attacks them.

Turtle Traits

Ye Olde Gentlemen

A lot of turtles can live longer than a hundred years. Adwaita, an Adabra Giant tortoise was the oldest known tortoise who died in Alipore Zoo, Kolkata, India in 2006 at the age of 255 years. Imagine, a tortoise who lived through all those drastic events in the world that happened in this time!

Galapagos Giant Tortoise

What's the difference between a Turtle and a Tortoise?

A tortoise is a turtle but not all turtles are tortoises. You can point out a tortoise if you see that:

- It's vegetarian (herbivorous).
- It's hidden-necked.
- It has a bigger and higher shell which is more domelike.
- It moves very slowly.
- Does not have webbed feet which other turtles have.

A Teeny Turtle

The smallest turtle in the world is a tortoise called the speckled padloper tortoise found in South Africa. It can grow only as long as 7 cm and be as light as 142 grams.

A group of turtles is called a bale. A bundle of straw bound tightly is also called a bale. Is there a connection?

Hidden-necked Turtle

Saving their Necks

Many turtles can tuck in their heads, legs and tails into their shells for protection. Turtles are separated into two groups based on the way they hide their necks. Those who take them back into their spine are called Cryptodira or Hidden-necked turtles. But those who turn the neck to one side and hide it under their shell are called Pleurodira or Side-necked turtles. Their necks are longer and their shells flatter.

The top part of the shell of a turtle is called the carapace while the bottom part is called the plastron. It is made up of 60 connected bones and have nerve endings too. That is why the shell of a turtle can feel your finger if you touch it.

Side-necked Turtle

Heavy Duty Shells

The shell of a box turtle is so strong that it can bear a weight that is 200 times heavier than the turtle.

Is it a Boy?...Or is it a Girl?

It takes two months for turtle eggs to hatch and whether it's a boy or a girl, it depends on the temperature. So if it's below 29 degrees Celsius, it's a boy, if it's above that, it's a girl!

No matter how hard it tries, a turtle can't leave its shell.

A Few Turtle Friends

Loggerhead Turtle

Loggerhead turtles are called so because they have large heads that look like big logs. They have strong jaws too with which they use to crush animals with hard shells.

Childhood Memories

Very often, female loggerhead turtles swim back thousands of kilometres to the beach where she herself hatched to lay her eggs.

Green Sea Turtle

The green sea turtle has flippers that look like paddles which make them excellent swimmers.

Leatherback Turtle

It is the world's largest turtle, can be more than 2m long and can weigh more than a ton!

Sea Sponge

Funny Food

Hawksbill turtles find highly poisonous sea sponges yummy, something that most animals can't afford to eat. Strange diet, isn't it?

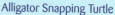

Snap and Sway the Turtle Way

The alligator snapping turtle looks like a rock and has a tongue that looks like a juicy worm. It happily sits at the bottom of a pond, waving its tongue with its mouth open. When an unsuspecting fish comes by, snap goes its mouth. A clever customer, eh?

Ugh!

The musk turtle is also known as stinkpot. If irritated, it gives out a stinky yellowish fluid.

Amphibians

Types of Amphibians

There are three types of amphibians—frogs and toads, salamanders and newts and caecilians.

What makes them special

- Have four legs
- Have moist and slimy or dry and warty skin
- Live near water.
- They differ from reptiles because their skins don't have scales and most of them go back to water to breed.

Frogs and Toads

- Bodies without necks.
- Have strong hind legs with which they leap.
- They swim with webbed feet.
- Have long tongues which are sticky with which they catch food.
- Lots of species found—around 3800.

Caecilians

- Their skin is smooth.
- They burrow like earthworms.
- Their jaws have teeth.
- Lesser number of species—around 75.

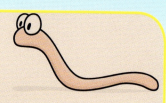

Salamanders and Newts

- Limbs weaker than frogs.
- Have a tail.
- Skin is smooth and moist with which they breathe oxygen.
- They have a neck.
- Average number of species—around 340.

Yellow Spotted Salamander

Frogs and Toads

A Frog's View

- My hind legs are long.
- I have smooth and moist skin.
- I like water and I like spending time in it.
- I leap.
- My upper jaw has teeth.
- My ears or tympanum are larger than a toad's.
- I have webbed feet.

A Toad's View

- My hind legs are short.
- My skin is rough and warty but I have other good qualities, you know.
- Water isn't my favourite hideout. So I don't spend a lot of time there
- My hops are short when I walk.
- I don't have teeth.
- You heard it from the braggart. Do I have to say that my ears are smaller?
- My hind feet are webless.

Cane Toad

The Well-Trodden Path

If you take a frog or toad away from their territory, they'll smell and use the position of the stars to find their way back. And a lot of species manage to come back every year wherever they are to the same breeding grounds.

Life Cycle of a Frog

1. A frog lays a bunch of her eggs (called a spawn) in water.
2. After hatching, the little frogs are known as tadpoles. They live in water, have a tail with which they swim and breathe through gills.

   Tadpoles who are very young, feed on the yoke of their egg which is still in their gut.
3. After a few weeks, their hind legs grow out and then their front ones.

   At that time, they also eat insects and plants.

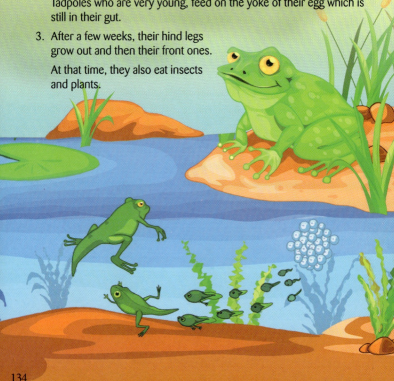

4. In the next stage, tadpoles become froglets. They start breathing with lungs, the legs are grown but there is still a bit of the tail left.
5. Of course, the next stop is land.
   As a full grown adult.

Lost in the Frog

The Amazon River alone has 1000 out of the 5000 species of frog. It's really froggy out there, isn't it?

Croak-a-doodle-doo!

The male Spring Peeper announces the arrival of spring by making sounds like sleigh-bells in a chorus.

The American Bullfrog's deep and loud sound is like the mooing of a cow and that explains why "bull" is included in its name. And yes, it can be heard a quarter of a mile away!

The Carpenter frog sounds like the hammering of nails by a carpenter.

Barking tree frogs bark like a pack of dogs who have gone on a hunt.

American Bullfrog

Spring Peeper

You Poisonous Toad…er…Frog!

The poison dart frog, who is only the size of a paper clip, is both beautiful and dangerous. The beautiful colours and venom are there to scare predators away. It is one of the most poisonous animals in the world and the venom in a golden poison dart frog is enough to kill 10 people. The Embera people of Colombia have tipped their darts with this poison for centuries for hunting.

The Best Offence is a Fashionable Defence

When it encounters a threat, the Oriental Fire-Bellied Toad stands up or sometimes topples over to show its bright belly with black spots. And because it is not bluffing, it even secretes a poison after this. To add to its fashion sense, its eyes have triangular pupils.

Don't Try This At Home

Wallace's Flying Frog, also known as parachute frogs, leap from branches, spread out their webbed feet and with the help of the webbing between their toes and spread skin flaps, can glide as far as 15m. Their large toe pads help them land softly or to stick to trees.

Shock Value

The red-eyed tree frog loves to shock its predators. When it feels threatened, it flashes its bright red eyes and uses its bright skin to confuse and dazzle the predator. This gives the frog time to make its escape to safety.

Salamanders

Female fire salamander about to be a mum.

Salamanders have bodies that are slender, long tails and a short nose. Like lizards they can grow back lost body parts, but unlike them, have no claws. Most of them have four toes in their front limbs and five at the back.

Barking Salamanders

Mudpuppies, also called waterdogs, as their name suggests, are the only salamanders who make a squeaky sound that reminds one of a dog's bark. You can make out a mudpuppy by the fact that it lives all its life underwater and by its red bushy gills which are on the outside. They grow up to be quite long for salamanders, averaging around 27 cm.

Mums with a Mission

The females of some species of salamanders are excellent mothers. They have been seen to curl up around their eggs to help them retain moisture in their shells. They also nudge their eggs to keep the inner membranes from sticking. Predators ought to be careful, for salamander mothers come to the defence of their eggs.

Female salamanders also have a way of identifying their own eggs if they're mixed up with others. This mechanism is in them most probably to stop them from eating their own eggs.

The Child Who Never Wanted to Grow Up

The axolotl salamander, found only in Mexico, remains a child even when it grows up. Its fin, that resembles a tadpole's, and external gills which it had as a larva pass on into adulthood. Unlike most other salamanders, it lives only in water.

Axolotl

Nothing the Newt

Red-spotted Newt

Newts are salamanders who usually live more of their adult lives in water compared to other salamanders and have flatter tails. They are found in moist woody areas of North America, Europe and Asia.

Protective Poison

The innocent-looking red spotted newt is not as innocent as it seems. It shows its bright colours to warn predators about its poisonous skin. True to itself, it does secrete poison when it's threatened or injured. Still, this is the most common pet newt. A really bad one is the rough skinned newt, who has enough poison to kill an adult human. Native Americans in the Pacific Northwest even use it to poison their enemies!

Warty yet Handsome

You would have seen really smooth and handsome princes in fairy tales. But even though the warty newt is covered with small bumps, their males in the mating season develop a smart crest along their backs which makes them look charming. And that is why it is also known as the great crested newt. Whoever said a person with warts cannot be Prince Charming?

New(t) Love!

A male newt works really hard to impress a female by showing off his brightly coloured skin.

Marine Animals

Did you know that more than two-thirds of the total area of the earth is covered by water? That's more than 70 per cent of the earth's surface! The ocean holds majority of the earth's living creatures, the number of species being somewhere between 500,000 to 10 million. Even some of the first dinosaurs to walk the earth lived, not on land, but in water!

Bizarre Beings

Most of the sea animals that we know of live in the upper layers of the oceans also called the sunlight zone. It was thought that life was not possible in the deep sea water. Today, we have discovered few, if not many, surviving in the deep waters of the oceans. And strange, they are! Some of these creatures have teeth as big as the size of their bodies, some have spines that prick and some have extremely big eyes, so big that they look as if they are going to pop out!

An Ocean of Life

Do you know that even a drop of sea water contains life forms? These creatures are so tiny that they cannot be seen by the human eye! But if you looked through a microscope at just a spoonful of sea water, you'd see hundreds of different tiny creatures swimming about. Huge masses of such creatures are called plankton. Plankton live in the upper layers of the oceans. This is because very little sunlight penetrates into the deep oceans and plankton need sunlight to grow. Plankton are a source of food for a great many sea creatures and in some cases, even for themselves.

Cold Fish

There are over 20,000 different kinds of fish, each with unique characteristics. Their bodies are filled with scales which help them glide through water easily, they have fins which help to steer and balance them, they breathe through gills and finally, they are cold-blooded animals. This means that their bodies stay at the same temperature as the sea.

Drink like a fish

Fish, like all animals need oxygen to breathe. You might be wondering why then are fish able to survive under water while humans are not. Well, when fish breathe, they take in the oxygen along with the water with the help of gills.

Floating Fish

Ever wondered why fish don't sink to the bottom of the ocean while gliding through the water? Well, fish have what acts like a balloon inside their bodies. This balloon contains air which helps them float under the water without them having to swim! Lucky fish!

A Fish Out of Water

Although all fish live in water and cannot survive without it, there are actually some fish that can survive on land. The mudskipper occasionally comes out of the water and hangs out on dry land. It can stay on land for short periods, as long as its body is moist and wet!

But nothing beats the lungfish! The lungfish can live on land by digging up a hole in the sand and burying itself in that hole when the water dries up during summer. It stays in that hole and waits for the rain to come. If the rains don't come, the lungfish can survive for up to four years without water!

What do fish eat?

All the animals in the sea depend on each other for food. Plant plankton is eaten by animal plankton, animal plankton is eaten by small fish and finally, the big fish eat the small fish. Sometimes, it can be the other way around where the small fish eat up the big fish. All in all, in the deep, deep sea, it's a fish eat fish world!

Fish spend all day searching for food. Different types of fish eat different food. And they have different and usually strange ways of acquiring it too!

Light-headed?

The angler fish has a light on its head. When curious fish go close to it to investigate the light, the angler fish surprises them by gobbling up the fish in one bite!

A Ball of Spines

With such highly evolved predators out there, one can never be too careful. That is why the porcupine fish has its whole body covered in spines. When it senses danger, this fish blows itself up so that the spines on his body stick out preventing predators from eating it. If you think this ball of spines is merciful, think again! These spines can be 5cm long and are extremely poisonous.

A Queer Fish

The cleaner shrimp is more benevolent in its approach. It feeds on the dead skin and parasites of the big fish. This way, the cleaner shrimp gets his meal and pays for it by giving its prey a good cleaning! Strange indeed!

Shoaling Around

There are many kinds of fish that swim together. These groups of fish are called shoals. Some fish are very social and prefer to have company as they go out hunting for food. A shoal can consist up to thousands of fish that all swim together and at the same speed. The most amazing thing noticed is that when the fish in front see danger and when they turn away, the fish behind also quickly follow suit. It appears as if they can read each other's minds.

A Sixth Sense

For fishes, senses play a highly important role when it comes to communication. Therefore, unlike all the rest of us, they have been blessed with the lateral line. This line can be seen along each side of the fish's body. Through this line, the fish is able to sense the movements of other fishes or animals in the water.

A Fish story

Scientists have classified fish into three broad categories. These are the jawless fish, the cartilaginous fish and the bony fish. The jawless fish appeared on earth 500 million years ago. There are only two existing species of the jawless fish today. They are the hagfish and the lamprey which are characterised by their jawless mouths. The sea lamprey has teeth and eats by sucking body fluids from its prey!

Inside Job

The hagfish is the most primitive fish in existence. It has an eel-like body, no scales and it looks nothing like fish. It has spots for eyes, only one nostril, has no backbone and is slimy. This fish is famous for its strange eating habit where, it burrows itself into the bodies of dead or injured animals and eats them from inside!

Gentle Giants

The next classification is the cartilaginous fish. This includes sharks, rays and skates. Such creatures have rows of razor-sharp teeth, scales, paired fins and their bodies have a skeleton, not of bone, but of cartilage.

Sharks

The worst thing that anyone can do while you're taking a dip in the sea or ocean is to simply yell out "shark!" and you're already in a state of panic. Whenever we think about sharks we think of big, menacing creatures that love to eat humans. Despite their reputation, not all sharks are dangerous. There are about 250 species of sharks and the biggest of them all, the whale shark, is completely harmless! In fact out of all the 250 species, only twelve are considered dangerous.

A Big Fish

Sharks come in all shapes and sizes. Sharks are fish but are very different from them in a number of ways. The most notable difference is the gills. A shark's gills look like slits and are open, unlike other fish. Also, a shark has denticles in place of scales. This makes the shark's skin feel rough. And, unlike the fish, the poor sharks don't have swim bladders. Therefore, they must keep swimming else, they will sink!

Head like a Hammer

Not all sharks are sleek and slender with razor-sharp teeth and streamlined bodies. The wobbegong and the angel fish have flat bodies and look nothing like sharks, much less like fish. The hammerhead has its own distinctive feature in its appearance. It has a head shaped like a hammer, which is where it got its name from, with huge bulging eyes at either end.

Shark Attack

Out of the twelve dangerous sharks out there, the great white shark and the tiger shark are the most dangerous. They feed on anything that comes their way, including rubbish! They eat large fish, seals, sea turtles and even humans. As hunters, they are adept. They have perfect eyesight, they can hear a fish under water a mile away and they can even smell a single drop of blood in the vast ocean!

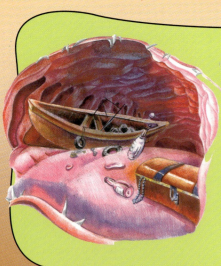

Cast iron Stomachs

Sharks do not chew their food. They simply bite their food and directly swallow it in. That is why scientists have found all sorts of things inside a shark's body. The skeleton of a horse, rubber tyres, nails, feathers, the skull of a cow and even a dog's bones have been found inside a shark's stomach.

Mermaids' Purses

While fish lay soft and wobbly eggs in huge numbers, sharks give birth to live baby sharks that learn to swim the minute they are born. There are of course, some sharks that do lay eggs. These shark eggs are hard and are encased in thick and strong leather cases which are called mermaids' purses. When the baby sharks are ready to come out, the eggs hatch and they swim out leaving the egg cases to be washed up on seashores.

On the Rocks

The wobbegong shark has an interesting way of acquiring its food. It lies low at the bottom of the ocean. It blends in so well in the seabed and is so well disguised that crabs and other fish crawl to it, thinking it's a rock. Suddenly, it opens its mouth and immediately shuts it and that's the end of the crab or fish!

Kith and Kin

Their close relatives, the rays and skates look nothing like the sharks. Their bodies are flat, unlike the sharks and they mostly live at the bottom of the sea. They have fins that look like wings and they flap them to swim. Rays have a number of different prints and patterns on their bodies. So, when they lie low at the bottom of the sea, hiding from sharks and other bigger rays, they are almost invisible!

Armed to the Snout

With its stomach on the seabed, the sawfish ray usually gets impatient waiting for its food. These sawfish rays, like the sawfish shark, have snouts that take the shape of a double-sided saw. With this saw, they disrupt the ocean floor, slash through shoals of fish and then feed on the ones injured or cut by its saw-like snout.

A Sting in the Tail

Now, the stingray's defence lies not on its snout but on its tail. This creature has a razor-sharp stinger at the end of its tail. This venomous stinger is about 35 cm and can sting humans as well as other creatures. Despite the toxin, the stingray is in fact a very docile creature, usually only using its sting to defend itself.

All Charged Up

Not only do rays have saws and stingers but some are also electrically charged. The torpedo ray can deliver up to 1,600 watts of power in one discharge! These rays use their electrical powers for self defence or even for catching prey.

A Different Kettle of Fish

And now, we have the fish that have both jaws and bones, and not cartilage. These are the bony fish. Each species varies in size and form. Scientists have found that there are 30,000 species of bony fish in the earth's oceans, each one extremely different from the other. The only thing, perhaps, that they have in common is the fact that they all have gills!

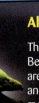

All Shapes and Sizes

These fishes come in different shapes and sizes. Besides the usual "cylindrical" shape of a fish, there are bony fishes that are flattened, like the goosefish and even longish, taking the shape of eels, like the morays.

The stonefish is a rather unusual looking creature. This fish takes the shape of a rock lying at the bottom of the sea. Therefore, when unsuspecting fish swim by, the stonefish opens its mouth and quickly gobbles it up!

Horse or Fish?

The seahorse too is a bony fish with an unusual shape for fish. It is called the sea horse because of its uncanny resemblance to horses. Its head resembles that of a horse and it has a curved tail. The most interesting fact about this creature is that baby sea horses hatch in their father's belly and not their mothers!

You Wouldn't Want This in Your Salad!

The seahorses' cousin, the sea dragon too, looks nothing like a fish. Nor does it look anything like the seahorse, despite them being cousins. It is leafy and when looked at closely resembles a dragon. Because they blend in so well with the environment, they have almost no predators!

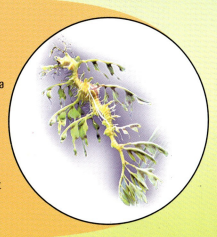

Fish in Scaly Armour?

Most bony fishes are covered by scales all over their bodies. These scales serve as the fishes' armour. They are made up of a flexible coating which protects them from predators, parasites and sharp rocks.

Can't Bat an Eyelid?

All fish, except for a few exceptions like sharks, rays, skates and a couple other, were born without eyelids. The goldfish, for instance, besides many other bony fishes, cannot close its eyes. They keep their eyes open even when they sleep!

Transformers, yet again!

Some fish can transform their shapes as they grow older. The flounder is one such fish. When the egg hatches, it comes out as an ordinary looking fish, of a cylindrical shape and with eyes on both sides of its head. As it begins to grow, it starts leaning on only one side of its body. Doing so, the eye on one side slowly migrates to the side with the other eye. This way, the fish goes through a most unusual transformation where, from becoming a cylindrical shaped fish, it becomes a flattened fish!

Changing Colours

Some species of fish can change colours. The colour of their bodies may change as the fish grows. In some cases, like the parrotfish, the baby parrotfish are always born as females. But as they grow older, some change to males. With their change in gender, they also change their colours.

Not totally different from us humans who blush or go red in the face when embarrassed, there are also some fish that change colour when stressed out!

Sink or Swim

While most bony fish sleep peacefully, some have to swim continually. The tuna has to swim even when it sleeps! This is because the tuna gets oxygen by swimming with its mouth open and letting the water and oxygen enter through it. It swims rapidly so that the oxygen quickly moves across its gills. If it stops swimming, it could suffocate and die!

Fighting Fish

Although most bony fish sound completely harmless, there are some who come out with a fighting stance and can be quite aggressive, quick to defend their territory and themselves. The damselfish usually like being alone and often quarrel with other damselfish when their territory is invaded.

The Siamese fighting fish too is extremely territorial. When a male Siamese fighting fish comes across another one, they fight each other till one gets seriously injured. Some even say that, if it sees its own reflection in a mirror, it would attack that too! No wonder the name, Siamese fighting fish.

All That Glitters…

The great barracuda has been known to attack humans. These creatures vary in size, the biggest reaching up to 2 metres and they have very long and sharp teeth. They are known for many attacks on divers, especially the ones that have a lot of shiny stuff on them. This is because they confuse the shiny objects with the shiny scales of their prey. They love bright and glittering things so the next time you want to go deep sea diving, you might want to leave your jewellery at home.

Small but Deadly

But the most vicious of all these are the piranhas. Piranhas are tiny creatures with scathing teeth that can bite through almost anything. They usually feed on smaller fish, but when there are no small fish, they can eat big sharks and humans. And that too, in minutes! When there are no small fish, no big sharks and no humans, they can attack anything that comes in their way, including other piranhas!

Food

The appetite of each bony fish differs from the next. Some are plant-eaters and some are meat-eaters while there are those that prefer to feed on the dead bodies of animals and on dead plants. Typically, most bony fish feed on clams, worms, mussels, plankton, squids, insects, birds and even animals.

Some fish prefer to eat throughout the day and some can go for long periods of time without any food. The freshwater eels can go on for a whole year without food!

Feeding on Scraps

Some bony fish have their own specialised ways of acquiring their prey. The remoras attach themselves to the fins of some other large creature like a shark and whenever the shark eats, they too get to feed on the leftover scraps.

Shooting Fish

An archer fish on the other hand, simply shoots at its prey. When it sees an insect buzzing, it quickly swims to the surface of the water and shoots out a stream of water from its mouth. The water hits the insect making it drop to the water and, jumping at the opportunity, the archer fish swims to it and immediately eats it up!

Marine Reptiles

Thick Skinned

Millions of years ago, terrifying reptiles ruled the oceans. These were the dinosaurs. Today, their descendant, the crocodile, one of the largest of all the living reptiles, lives on both land and water. Like their ancestors, these creatures are heavily armoured. They are covered with a thick impenetrable coat of scales. These scales are in turn made of horn and the hide is so thick that spears as well as arrows can't shoot through it.

Bullet Proof?

Some believe that the hide of a crocodile is so thick that even bullets can't penetrate it. This is in fact more of a myth than a fact. A crocodile is hardly safe from bullets. The only things that would protect them are the bony plates under their skin. It is true that a large, full grown crocodile can survive a shot or two from a smaller caliber gun. However, a few well-aimed shots to their vital areas from a larger gun would definitely bring it down.

Did you Know...

Crocodiles eat anything that comes their way. But if no food comes along, they can go on without eating for months. They sometimes eat stones because it helps them to digest their food easily.

Bearing Arms

In addition to it being heavily armoured, the crocodile is also heavily armed. It has a long snout, which when opened, shows off 24 sharp and powerful teeth that can crush bones and a powerful jaw. Besides this, it has a strong and powerful tail that can snap a small tree with one blow!

Crocodile Tears

Legend has it that when a crocodile feeds on a human being, it weeps. This is because when crocodiles eat, they devour the meal so much that their eyes water with froth and bubble during the feeding!

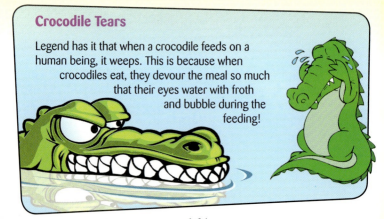

Floatin' like a Log

Crocodiles don't go out hunting for their prey. They wait for the prey to come to them. That is why you see them lying low in shallow waters looking pretty much like logs floating in the water. This is how they catch unsuspecting animals or people. So, the next time you see a log floating in shallow water, try not to go too close. It might be our friend, the crocodile!

Fierce Man-Eaters

And sometimes these creatures like to sink their teeth into humans too! Although they are not aggressive creatures by nature, they can however be easily provoked, especially the female crocodiles that are busy mothering their newborns. The saltwater crocodile is believed to be the only crocodile most likely to gobble up a human. These creatures are fierce and massive and are the largest of the crocodilian family reaching up to a height of 5 meters!

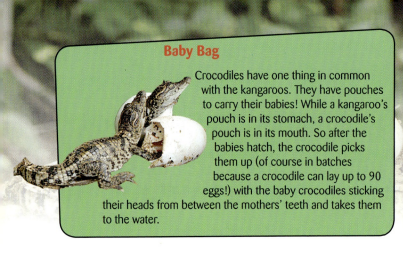

Baby Bag

Crocodiles have one thing in common with the kangaroos. They have pouches to carry their babies! While a kangaroo's pouch is in its stomach, a crocodile's pouch is in its mouth. So after the babies hatch, the crocodile picks them up (of course in batches because a crocodile can lay up to 90 eggs!) with the baby crocodiles sticking their heads from between the mothers' teeth and takes them to the water.

Sea or Land Creatures?

Found only in the Galapagos Islands, the marine iguana is the only lizard that can adapt itself to both land and water. Not all lizards can do this. While on land, this lizard can be clumsy and awkward, in the sea, it swims gracefully.

All Powdered up

Marine iguanas, like humans, are usually found with powder on their faces, most of the time, too much. While humans powder themselves intentionally the marine iguana knows nothing of this trend. Because they spend so much time in the sea, the content of salt is extremely high in their bodies. Basking in the sun helps them to remove the salt from their bodies which they then sneeze out. This is why marine iguanas often look all powdered and puffed up!

Sea snakes

Another scaly friend that thrives in water is the sea snake. This creature is the most venomous of all the snakes. The most poisonous of the whole lot is the beaked sea snake. Scientists claim that only three drops of its venom can kill about eight people. Sea snakes can survive up to an hour under water. They have a paddle-like tail which helps them swim fast.

Did you Know...

Sea snakes are very fussy eaters. Some eat only catfish, some only eels and some only fish eggs.

Shy Snake?

Sea snakes are generally very shy. They prefer hiding in some corner when they see intruders. They are not usually aggressive. The banded sea snake is one of the shy ones. It does not attack divers or other creatures unless it plans on eating them!

Sea Turtles

The most interesting out of all the sea reptiles are the sea turtles and tortoises with their graceful countenance. These creatures may be slow, sluggish and clumsy on land but in water, they show skill and ability, despite some weighing up to even 225 kg and more!

Soft on the Inside and Hard on the Outside

It has a soft body with a hard armour-like shell around it, similar to the land turtles except for its flippers that help it dive down into deep oceans. It can't however, retract its body into its shell like the land turtles.

There are strange markings on a sea turtle's shell. An old, ancient culture that existed years and years ago believed that these markings predicted when the world would come to an end.

Nomads

While it spends most of its time underwater, it comes out whenever it needs to breathe or to lay eggs. This means that baby sea turtles and males hardly come to shore. They travel for most of their lives in search of warmer waters. The Loggerhead travels about 1500 km from ocean to ocean for better nesting sites.

Did you Know...

A female sea turtle can lay upto 200 eggs at one time.

Sea Birds

There are also creatures that don't live on just land and water. These can fly, swim and walk as well. Out of more than eight thousand species of birds, there are a few that can do all this. Besides having feathers for flying, these birds have webbed feet that help them to paddle under water. Some even use their feathers to help them dive underwater. Sea birds are excellent sea divers. The emperor penguin can dive to depths of up to around 250 meters!

Headbanger

Sea birds feed on fish which they acquire by diving into the sea. The kingfisher usually spends much of its time sitting on a branch watching the water for fish to feed on. When it sees one, it instantly dives into the water and seizes it in its mouth. Once the bird has it in its mouth, it quickly flies back to the branch, knocks out the fish by banging its head on the branch, tosses it into the air, catches it with its beak and gobbles it up!

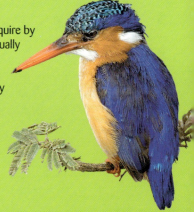

Skilled Fishermen

More than using their wings for flying, the puffin uses them more for swimming. It prefers to stay in water rather than in the sky. It has a comical appearance and is a favourite for many. A puffin has the ability to catch up to five or six fish, one at a time. What amazes us is its ability to hold on to one fish while it catches another!

Bottoms Up

Ducks have different ways of acquiring their prey. They stand upside down in such a way that their heads are underwater and their feet and tails stick straight up in the air!

Wings but Can't Fly?

What has the body shape of a fish, head and beak of a bird and wings but can't fly? A penguin, of course, one of the most well-loved of all the sea birds. It champions as an underwater swimming bird and spends most of its time at sea. Penguins are found in icy cold regions and in order to be able to stand the cold, have a thick layer of fat called the blubber along with waterproof feathers to keep them warm.

Pouch in the Mouth

The pelicans are of a different kind altogether. They are large water birds with pouches on their beaks. With this pouch they scoop fish swimming near the surface of the water. Then they drain out the water and swallow the fish!

Leafy Rafts

The most unusual out of all the sea birds however is the grebes. People often call them water witches because of their skill at swimming. These creatures build their nests underwater. These nests are made of decayed plants that help them float on water. These rafts are fastened with cattails and weed stalks.

Sea Mammals

The largest of all the sea animals are the whales. These creatures look like huge fish but in fact they are mammals; they breathe air and are warm-blooded creatures. This means that their bodies remain warm even if the sea is cold. Whales breathe air just as we humans and often have to come to the surface for air every 5-7 minutes. If they stay underwater for too long, they can drown!

Toothless

Some whales don't have teeth. Whales like the baleen whales have baleen instead of teeth. This baleen acts as a strainer which helps them to filter out food from the water. The baleen whales, like the humpback whale, take in large gulps of water and then sift the water out through their baleen, taking in only the krill. But of course, since the krill are so small, The blue whale can eat about 6000 kg of it per day!

Whoosh

Whales have an opening at the top of their heads called the blowhole. When they dive back to the surface to breathe, there's always some air left in the windpipe and they need to get rid of it so that they can take a fresh breath of air. They simply squirt out this air through the blowhole and whoosh it shoots out.

Meat-eaters

As for the whales that do have teeth, they have really sharp ones. These whales are usually meat-eaters and eat fish and squid. Narwhals and bottlenoses eat crabs and lobsters. The killer whales go for much bigger animals like the seals and porpoises. Sometimes, these creatures have even attacked humans. But that's only because they have such poor eyesight and when they see a diver in the deep ocean, they usually think it's a seal!

Mammoth Mammals

The blue whale is the largest mammal in the world. It measures up to 30m and weighs about 200,000 kg. That means that it is as long as two school buses put together and weighs about the same as ten school buses! Its heart is as heavy as a helicopter and its tongue can weigh as much as a fully grown elephant!

The blue whales, like us humans, give birth to live young. Because their mothers are so big, it is expected that the young they give birth to, should also be big. The blue whale babies emerge measuring about 7m and 3000 kg!

Brainy Whale

If you've read Moby Dick then you'll certainly be familiar with this one. It is grey and large and is one of the few toothed whales. This whale holds the record for having the largest brain in the animal world. Its brain alone weighs about 9 kg!

Singing Whale

With the reputation of being the most playful of the whales, the male humpback has been heard singing loudly as it dives underwater. This whale, it has been observed, usually sings when he is in the company of another female humpback. This has led researchers to believe that they sing to woo or to get the attention of the female humpbacks.

Flashing a Smile

The dolphins and the porpoises are cousins of whales. Their bodies are shaped the same way but they are much smaller compared to the whales. Dolphins have proven to be one of the most playful and friendliest creatures in the sea. They have a beak-like snout that makes them look as if they are smiling. Not only this, when they actually do smile, they show off about a hundred coned teeth which they don't even use!

Backscratcher

While they have so many teeth, it is quite a wonder why these creatures choose not to chew their food but rather swallow it whole. This is because they have other uses for their teeth. Since they move around in pods, they use their teeth for scratching each other's backs!

Keeping an Eye Out

Dolphins don't sleep! Well they do but only with one eye closed. The other eye is usually kept open even as they sleep. This is because, by keeping one eye open, the dolphin is keeping a part of its brain active. With one eye and part of the brain active, the creatures can keep an eye out for predators.

Porpoises

The porpoises are a lot like dolphins. Their difference is marked by their rounded snout, unlike the beak-like snouts of the dolphins. They are fast swimmers and are often seen taking free rides on the bow waves of passing ships.

Whiskered Friends

The seals, the sea lions and the walruses are mammals too that live underwater. As a group they are called pinnipeds which means fin foot because they have flippers for feet. They can survive underwater and on land as well. While their bodies are streamlined for swimming, on land they waddle about on fins. Big creatures of the oceans like sharks and whales feed on them.

Vanity Fair?

The sea otters are furry and adorable looking creatures, the smallest amongst the marine mammals. They spend most of their time in water, swimming on their backs. Their fur has been considered to be the finest in the animal kingdom. And the sea otters know it too! That is why they spend more than half of each day grooming their fur. The sea otters in fact have to care for their fur, without which, they wouldn't survive. This is because these creatures don't have blubber like most marine mammals. They therefore depend on their thick fur to keep them warm.

Swimming Bears

The Polar Bear is also a mammal that has adapted to life on both land and water. This creature lives close to the North Pole where the temperature is icy cold. The polar bears are strong swimmers and can hunt for their prey – seals and many other creatures – both on land and in water!

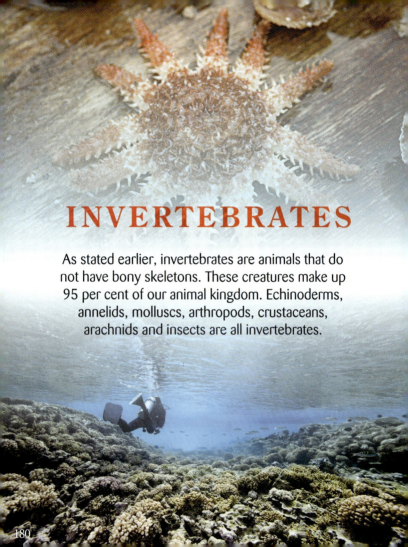

INVERTEBRATES

As stated earlier, invertebrates are animals that do not have bony skeletons. These creatures make up 95 per cent of our animal kingdom. Echinoderms, annelids, molluscs, arthropods, crustaceans, arachnids and insects are all invertebrates.

Invertebrates

One of the largest groups in the animal kingdom is that of the invertebrates. They have no backbone and have soft gooey bodies without any bone structure; some have only shells to protect them.

An Umbrella Made of Jelly?

What do you call a creature that looks like an umbrella made of jelly? You call it a jellyfish!

Did you know that the jellyfish is not even a fish, despite its name? It belongs to the family of invertebrates. This strange creature comes in all colours – white, pink and blue and in all sizes too! Some are even transparent and glow in the dark!

Sea monsters

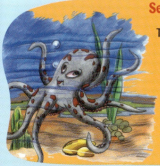

The octopus, which belongs to the family of molluscs, has eight snake-like arms and a head with eyes on either side. This creature does not have an outer shell and uses its eight long arms, which are called tentacles to feed on its prey. Each tentacle has up to two hundred and twenty suction cups by which it sucks its prey into.

Why do Squids Squirt Ink?

The squid too is another sea creature with eight to ten arms and two tentacles on their heads. Squids excrete an ink-like fluid from their bodies which makes it impossible for the predator to see through, giving way to its escape. The giant squid is the biggest of the squids and can grow up to ten meters long!

Slippery Feet

Slugs and snails produce a thick coat of slime from their feet especially when in danger. This shine gives an unpleasant taste to the coating to ward off potential predators.

Oysters

Oysters are molluscs that live in a shell. These creatures have gills and breathe just as fishes do. Oysters evolved when a tiny crab went to live inside an oyster shell and decided to make it its home. The most interesting feature about the oyster, which is why it is highly valued by humans, is that it produces pearls. When a piece of grit enters the shell, these crabs secrete a kind of substance which in time hardens and soon becomes a pearl.

Crabwise

Crabs too have a hard shell and ten legs like the lobsters and the shrimps. But unlike the other two, the crab's body is flattened. A notable feature of a crab is the fact that it walks sideways! This is because of the way a crabs' legs are formed. While a crab can move backwards as well as forwards, it can only move fast if it walks sideways. Therefore, when it has to escape from predators, it needs to walk fast, in this case, sideways.

Did you know...

Like the oysters, even mussels and clams can make pearls too.

As Happy as a Clam

Have you ever seen something that looks like two sea shells hinged together? These creatures are called clams. Clams come from the family of mussels. Inside the shells is a soft bodied creature. Whenever the clam wants to move, it simply takes out its foot and pushes it forward as you would do a paddle.

Swimming Backwards

The cuttlefish has its shell inside its body. Inside the shell, there is a bubble of gas which helps it to float under water. Its swims backwards and can change its colours in an instant, even faster than a chameleon! They change colours to prevent hunters from seeing them.

Curiosity Killed the Cat…

While clams are usually small, the giant clam can grow up to 2m! These creatures are the biggest molluscs in the world. While clams usually eat plankton, some believe that the giant clam eats people too. This is in fact not true as meat is not part of a clam's diet. However, an incident occurred once that a man went close to a giant clam which had its shell open. The giant clam sensed the intruder and immediately shut its shell with a mighty snap which seriously injured him.

Ten-Legged Creatures

Lobsters have gills like fish, hard shells, ten legs and four feelers. They use eight of their legs for walking and the other two are used as arms with fierce-looking pincers. The shrimps too look a lot like the lobsters, just smaller. Some of them are so small that they can't be seen without a microscope!

Ocean Floor

And at the very bottom of the sea which is called the seafloor, we find a breathtaking display of unique creatures like sea anemones, sea cucumbers, tube worms, clams and many more that thrive on whatever falls down from above. At the bottom of the sea, they feed on all types of creatures that crawl on the seabed.

Seeing Stars

If you think that there are stars only in the sky, think again! Deep in the oceans, we have beautiful star shaped creatures, of many different colours called starfish. If a starfish loses an arm, it simply grows a new one. In fact, if a starfish is torn into two, each part grows into a new starfish!

Sunstars too!

Similar to the starfish, but with more arms, the sunstars crawl over the seabed hunting for prey all day long. They feed on shellfish and starfish too!

Sea Cucumbers

What looks like a cucumber with feet and can be found in the deep oceans, most of the time on the ocean floor, at times, even half buried under the sand? Why, a sea cucumber, of course! These creatures do not grow in gardens but stay deep in the oceans and feed on algae and other tiny creatures that crawl on the seabed.

Sea Urchins

Sea urchins are ball-shaped creatures covered with spines that look like pins all over their bodies. These animals hide in openings and cracks between rocks.

Bottom Dollars?

Sand dollars are believed to be money that mermaids use, but they are living animals. They have flat bodies that look like round white coins. Instead of arms, like those of the starfish, sand dollars have pores under their bodies that help them to move around.

Invertebrates have no eyes, no brains and no hearts. Yet, they are breathing, living animals. These creatures look so different from all other sea animals. They need to eat and breathe just as we humans and animals do and are animals, just as animal as the tigers and the lions around us.

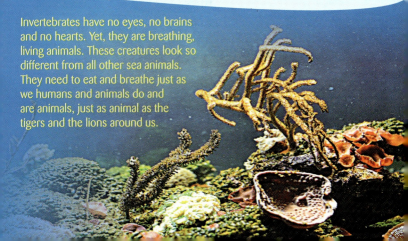

Six-legged Creatures

Insects are creatures that have six legs. Scorpions and spiders have more than six legs therefore, they are not insects. Flies, bees, ants, beetles, butterflies, crickets and grasshoppers all have six legs and therefore are all part of the insect family. Besides six legs, they have two feelers. Some insects have wings too, few have a pair and others have two pairs.

Here, There and Everywhere

As much as we humans have tried to stay away from insects, they just keep coming! There are more than one million kinds of insects breeding in this world; thousands are probably sitting somewhere close to you. In fact, there are more insects in one neighbourhood than there are humans in the world! Just the ladybird alone has about 4000 different known species out.

Eyes

An insect has hundreds of tiny eyes in each eye. Dragonflies have the most number of lenses in their eyes. The number of lenses that each dragon fly can have can go up to 30,000 lenses while we humans have only one!

Smell and Taste

Not only this, most insects don't have tongues. Flies taste with their feet! Unlike us humans and almost all creatures of the animal world, flies simply walk over something if they want to taste it. A fly's sense of smell is way sharper than that of humans, yet they have no noses. How is this possible? Well, they smell with their feelers at the top of their heads!

Don't let the Bed Bugs Bite

Bed bugs only bite at night and stay hidden during the daytime. As the name suggests, they usually hide in mattresses and come out for their feeding while you're asleep. Straight away after feeding, these flat insects become rounded. They are usually harmless, except for the irritating itchy feeling that they leave behind.

Not many humans like insects. They are crawly, creepy creatures that are not pleasant to look at and to top the list, they bite, they sting, and they stink too!

Flea Bag

If you're an animal lover, you'd definitely know what fleas are and where they come from. Fleas are insects that we find in the coats of dogs and cats, so when you see your pet scratching itself, there's probably a flea on its hair. While they usually bite the animal on whose coats they keep themselves warm, they can sometimes bite humans too!

Busy Bees

Bees are also scary insects that sting humans. While bees like to keep themselves busy making honey, they get upset if someone gets in their way and they can cause trouble. When a bee stings, the pain usually feels like a needle is piercing through your skin. While most stings are harmless, some can even be fatal. In fact, it has been proven that more people have died from bee stings than from snake bites or even shark attacks!

Frightening Feet

But the worst from the lot is the common house fly. This insect flies from one place to another and at a fast speed too. Since they taste food by walking over it, they end up tasting all kinds of adulterated and rotting foods and plants, thereby collecting germs on their feet. Then, they come to your home, inside your kitchen and walk over your clean food. The germs it might have carried from the previous place ultimately get transferred to your food and eventually to you after you have eaten it! The house fly is in fact a carrier of the most dangerous diseases in the world, including malaria.

Smelly Bugs

Stink bugs, like the name suggests, release an unpleasant odour when you crush them or when they are protecting their homes.

Making Homes

Not all insects hide away in animal hair or thick mattresses. Some prefer to build their own homes like the bees and the hornet. Bees make their own hives from wax that comes out of their bodies. They build one hive for each bee, the whole hive is run by the Queen bee and the rest are her workers

Paper Palaces

The hornet builds its home by pecking on a tiny piece of bark from a tree and chews it till it becomes a wet paste. Then, the hornet sticks the paste under a branch which then dries into a kind of paper. It continues on doing so until it has built a small cup. It then continues making the cups, all joined together. This is where the hornet lays its eggs.

Survivors

The cockroach, the oldest of the insects, isn't really choosy when it comes to a place to stay. It can survive anywhere be it at the top of a cold mountain or in the middle of the rainforest

Termite Towers

Like their relatives, the bees and the hornet, termites too build their own houses. The only difference is probably that the houses that termites build are ten, sometimes even twenty times the size of those of the bees and the hornets! These creatures build huge towers that house millions of termites. This tower, or rather city is hard, like a rock and has hundreds of tunnels and rooms inside of it. It is ruled by a king and a queen. The rest of the population are soldiers that guard and protect the king and queen and the workers that strive everyday at building the city. The queen of a termite colony may lay up thousands eggs per day, and may live as long as 15 to 50 years.

Ladybirds to the Rescue

As much as we dislike insects, not all of them are bad. While we constantly fume over the fact that one third of the earths crops get eaten and destroyed by insects, there are those that come to our rescue. The ladybirds feed on insects that feed on and destroy many kinds of plants that we use for food. Farmers use different types of chemicals to kill these insects so as to prevent them from destroying the plants. When all hope fails, we can depend on our friends, the ladybirds.

Making all the Right Noises

Since times immemorial, people have depended on the sounds that crickets make to be able to predict the weather. Their chirps differ just as the weather changes.

Metamorphosis

We may think of insects as ugly, creepy, crawly creatures, but never when it comes to the butterflies. Butterflies are the most beautiful of insects. They come in all different colours and sizes. But did you know that the butterfly was one as creepy and crawly as all the other insects. It was once a caterpillar! This process by which a caterpillar changes into a butterfly is called metamorphosis.

Changing Colours

Head lice can change their colours to the colour of the hair of the person whose hair they are living in.

An Army on its Stomach

Army ants usually move around in large numbers. Sometimes, their numbers get so large that a whole army of these insects consists of millions. Army ants have actually once caused the excavation of an entire village because it was so large in number!

Glow in the Dark

Fireflies are not flies but beetles. Just as beetles, they have hard wing covers. The most interesting part about then is the fact that they glow in the dark. Fireflies are often seen dancing under the night sky, all lighted up, and fluttering their wings about. Well, it is usually the males who do this as a sign of mating. They shine their light at the female fireflies and if the ladies are interested, they flash their light right back at them.

Arachnids

Along Came a Spider

Spiders, as mentioned in the earlier chapters, are not insects. These creatures belong to the family of arachnids. There are as many as 40,000 species of spiders out there. They have many eyes and walk on eight legs that grow each time one breaks!

Arachnophobia!!!

Many people are terrified of spiders. In fact, so many people are afraid of them that experts have even given that fear a name. The fear of spiders has been termed as arachnophobia. This term of course not only refers to the fear of spiders but to all other arachnids including scorpions.

A Death Trap

Spiders are just as busy as the bees when it comes to working. They weave their cobwebs every single day. Spider webs are in fact traps set up so that the spider can catch its prey. This spider web is made of a special silk thread that is produced out of their bodies and is sticky. Therefore, when an insect flies into a spider web, it gets caught in the strands and the spider gets its meal!

Jumping Jacks

However, not all spiders weave webs. Some species like the jumping spider waits for its prey by sitting on a plant or flower and waiting for an insect to come. As soon as it spots one, it immediately jumps on it and gobbles it up!

Predators

Spiders are predators and eat all kinds of insects. They eat flies, bees, wasps, ants, crickets, grasshoppers, beetles, bugs, including creatures that harm our crops. The bigger ones even eat small birds and lizards. And while they eat many creatures, many other creatures like to eat them too! Birds, mammals, reptiles, amphibians and fish all enjoy spiders for lunch.

All spiders have two fangs with which they inject venom into the bodies of their prey or enemies. However, not all spiders are dangerous. In fact, spiders are rather timid creatures and only attack when provoked. Also, some spider bites are practically harmless!

Tarantula

Of course there are those that are harmless. The black widow spider and the red-back spider are considered to be the two most dangerous spiders and their bite could be fatal. The tarantula's bites, however, most feared by people can only be as dangerous as a bee sting. Go figure!

Stinging Tail

Now the scorpions are also part of the family of arachnids, just as dangerous as their relative, the spider. Scorpions also have eight legs. In the place of fangs, they have a long, jointed tail which has a sting at the tip. A scorpion's sting is supposed to be highly poisonous and can be fatal if not treated.

Mites and Ticks

Another two species of arachnids are mites and ticks. These creatures are parasites that use their jaws to suck blood from other animals. They usually thrive on the bodies of animals that have a coat of hair, where they can remain unseen and protected.

Worms

Earthworms

If we turn over a little soil with a shovel, we find a great number of creatures. One such creature that burrows itself in the deep soil is the earthworm. It lives underground and only comes to the surface when it rains. It has a long cylindrical body, no legs, no arms, no eyes and it can't hear too! It is slimy, wiggly, slithery and creepy and not many people would want to go near it.

Apple Worm?

The codling moth is famous for causing a lot of damage to apple orchards. It lays its eggs on the leaves of the apple and when they hatch, they grow into tiny little worms. These worms burrow into the fruit which they contentedly chomp away. Then, when the fruit falls, the worms leave the apple and grow into codling moths which later on go to lay their eggs on the leaves of the apple trees.

A Hundred Legs

The word 'centipede' means a hundred legs. Despite their name, not all centipedes have a hundred legs. The house centipede, like most other species of this kind, actually has about fifteen to twenty pairs of legs while the Geophilus carpophagus has one hundred and seventy seven pairs!

Night Creepers

It is not very difficult to spot centipedes around the house. They have flat bodies about an inch long, two antennae and long legs that help them run fast. These creatures like to stay in dark places like woodlands, under leaves and logs. Around the house, they stay in dark corners and basements. They only like to come out at night in search for their prey. They feed on animals such as mice and different types of insects which they stun with their venomous jaws.

A Thousand Legs?

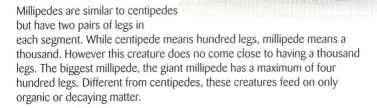

Millipedes are similar to centipedes but have two pairs of legs in each segment. While centipede means hundred legs, millipede means a thousand. However this creature does no come close to having a thousand legs. The biggest millipede, the giant millipede has a maximum of four hundred legs. Different from centipedes, these creatures feed on only organic or decaying matter.

Kicking up a Stink

Millipedes are not predators so are therefore hunted upon by other creatures. To protect themselves, this creature rolls itself up into a tight coil and oozes a foul smelling liquid that scares off any predators.

EXTINCT AND ENDANGERED SPECIES AND CONSERVATION

At present, Earth is a planet which has the right conditions for developing and sustaining life. We are not sure that these conditions will continue for many more years. Human activity can change the conditions on earth forever.

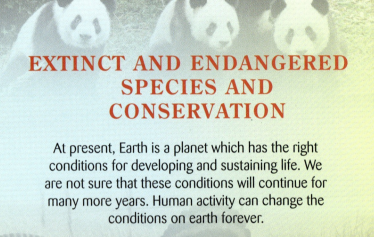

World's Great Mysteries

Towards the close of the 19th century, enormous bones of a creature that looked like those of a gigantic lizard were dug up. Scientists were baffled. They called it the "dinosaur" which means "terrible lizard." Since then, scientists all over the world have worked at finding out about this mysterious creature. They had discovered the dinosaur!

More dinosaur bones were excavated around the world. Today, millions and millions of years after their extinction, we are still digging and finding out clues about them.

Do you know how old our planet is? It is more than 4 billion years old! And how do we know that? From the dinosaurs! Not that they ever came to tell us so, but when the scientists discovered how old the dinosaurs are, they consequently found out how old the earth is. We humans only appeared on earth about three million years ago.

These scientists who study prehistoric life including that of the dinosaurs and many other animate beings that existed a long time ago and are extinct today are called palaeontologists. Through years of study, these palaeontologists have discovered that the "dinosaur" was in fact no lizard. Most of them were not even terrible.

What are fossils?

Fossils are the remains of animals that died a long time ago. When an animal dies, the soft part of its body rots away leaving only the bones. These bones, through time get covered by mud, sand, dust, etc. Over time, the earth's soil has special minerals that turn the bones into stone, thus making it a fossil!

Palaeontologists have found fossils of all kinds of dinosaurs of all shapes and sizes. They also found fossils of dinosaur eggs which they have preserved in museums around the world.

They have also found fossils that had the imprint of a dinosaur's footprints!

Before the dinosaurs, palaeontologists have found that there were creatures called the trilobites. These were small creatures that lived in the sea.

The period called the Mesozoic era was the age of the dinosaurs. This era can be split into three different periods – the Triassic period, the Jurassic period and the cretaceous period.

During the Triassic period, creatures like the Ichthyosaurs had ruled the earth. It lived on fish and ancient squid, and resembled the shape of a dolphin and could leap like dolphins too.

Another giant-sized reptile that lived during this age is the plesiosaurs. It had a long neck and large flippers. Both the ichthyosaurs and the plesiosaurs were sea reptiles and had long, smooth bodies that helped them to move under water.

And then were the flying reptiles like the pterosaurs. These creatures are very much like the bats of today. They had sharp teeth, wings and very light bones.

One of the most popular that lived during this period was the Plateosaurus. It was enormous, its size measuring up to twenty seven feet long! Its tail made up half of its body length, its legs looked like pillars, and it walked on all fours unlike the dinosaurs that followed. This creature belonged to the Triassic period, lived on plants and fell prey to many other animals that lived during that era.

Following the Triassic period was the Jurassic period. This period was dominated by dinosaurs on land. They were big, fierce and they were meat-eaters. Allosaurus was one of the dominant species who lived during that time. This creature fed on smaller and weaker dinosaurs and mammals. It walked on two feet, had sharp teeth and claws making him a strong and fierce predator.

It was during the Jurassic age where the first bird, the archaeopteryx came into existence. These birds evolved from dinosaurs, they had feathers and wings for flying.

Fifty five million years later, the Jurassic age came to an end and what followed was the Cretaceous period. This age was marked with the existence of the Triceratops, which had sharp horns to keep enemies away. This creature was a herbivore and lived in herds.

T-Rex had sharp teeth and was one of the fiercest meat eaters that ever existed. Evidence shows that Tyrannosaurus was about 12m long with strong legs and could eat up to 226 kg of meat in one bite! Not only this, it has a strong and powerful jaw that can crush bones with one snap! Tyrannosaurus Rex was one of the last dinosaurs to have walked the earth.

Larger than this mighty creature was Spinosaurus. Spinosaurus is actually the largest dinosaur to have ever existed. This creature had a sail on its back and an unusually long and narrow head.

Towards the later Cretaceous period, a dinosaur called Euoplocephalus existed. Euoplocephalus was a heavy armoured dinosaur whose body was covered with bony plates and spikes. It was the size of a small elephant and its most distinctive feature was its tail. It had a club-like tail which it used to defend itself.

Parasaurolophus also lived during the Late Cretaceous period. Its fossils show that it had a bony beak which helped it to tear off plants for eating. Another feature was the bony crest on its head.

Did you know?

Dinosaurs usually move in herds and within that herd they keep a leader. That is why they fought with each other to be able to claim that title.

The dinosaurs died about sixty five million years ago. No one knows exactly why they became extinct. Research shows that an asteroid could have hit the earth at that period. Also, there were many volcanic eruptions and the world was becoming really cold. It could have been any of these reasons that caused the dinosaurs to die out and made life on earth impossible.

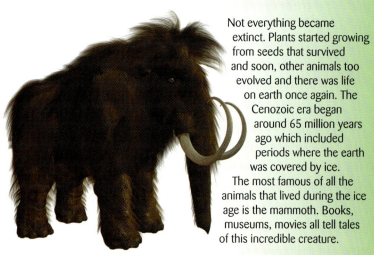

Not everything became extinct. Plants started growing from seeds that survived and soon, other animals too evolved and there was life on earth once again. The Cenozoic era began around 65 million years ago which included periods where the earth was covered by ice. The most famous of all the animals that lived during the ice age is the mammoth. Books, museums, movies all tell tales of this incredible creature.

Another distant relative of the mammoth is the mastodon. This creature lived during the same period as the mammoth and is also a distant relative of the elephant family. The mastodon looked much like the elephants that we have today, except for the thick coat of fur on its back, similar to that of the mammoth. They had pointy wide teeth, perfect for eating plants. They became extinct only about 10,000 years ago, which scientists believed, was due to climate change or over hunting by humans.

The sabre tooth cat had large, sabre-like canine teeth which extended outside of their mouths even when closed. Their tail is short and small. They were the most successful predators during that period. They behaved like members of the feline family, but are different from them in many respects. In fact, these ferocious, meat-eating animals are believed to be more closely related to kangaroos than to felines.

Probably one of the most interesting and mysterious birds to have walked the earth is the dodo. The dodo is believed to have belonged to the family of pigeons. It had a large, hooked beak and was found in the island of Mauritius. When people started coming into Mauritius and as the population grew. They started hunting them down. Forests were being cut down thereby destroying their habitats. By the 17th century, this bird was no where to be seen.

Did you know…

The dodo was considered dumb by many people during its age because its friendly nature to humans and predators alike made them easy targets.

The Giant Moa was a fascinating creature. The Giant moa was a flightless bird and the tallest bird to have ever walked the earth. It was considerably taller than the ostrich and weighed about 250 kg. These interesting creatures were found in many parts of New Zealand. But with the flooding in of colonists, they were driven into extinction due to farming, deforestation and even hunting till they became completely wiped out by the year 1500.

Only about sixty five years extinct, the Tasmanian wolf looked like a dog, acted like a wolf but was a relative of the kangaroos and the wombats. During that time, Tasmania had highly encouraged agriculture. The Tasmanian wolf was considered a threat to the livestock. Therefore, people started killing these creatures till they finally became extinct in the 20th century.

There are over 5000 known species of animals that are at risk of facing extinction in the Earth today. The main danger to their lives comes from people who damage and change the environments in which they live.

Deforestation is the cutting and clearing of trees in the forest and is one of the main causes of animal extinction today. People clear forests for agriculture, logging, mining, oil and gas extraction and many other purposes. The forest is home to millions of species of animals and each year a large area of the forest gets cut down. This means that with each forest being cleared, thousands or even millions of animals are being deprived of their homes. Animals need homes the same way that we humans do and with their homes being destroyed, most are unable to survive.

Not all deforestation is however intentional. In some cases, forests have been destroyed by wildfires. Wildfires can be caused by many natural occurrences such as lightning, volcanic eruptions and underground coal fires besides many others. But they can also sometimes be caused by human carelessness while handling fireworks or by starting campfires and not putting the fire off after use.

Another cause of deforestation is overgrazing. This can occur when plants are exposed to too much grazing without being given enough time to recover. When land is being overgrazed, its productivity and usefulness lessens and usually this leads to erosion and desertification.

Deforestation also brings about climate change. While forests are usually wet and damp, without the trees, there would be no shade to protect the plants from the sun, therefore, they quickly dry out.

Another cause of the extinction of animals is the hunting and tapping of animals for profit. Millions of animals are killed by hunters for selling its body parts which are usually considered valuable and are highly priced. The elephant tusk, since long, from the time of the ancient Egyptians, has been considered valuable. These are used for ornamental carvings, figurines, piano keys, dominoes and even false teeth.

Fur has been considered as one of the most luxurious of clothing – fur coats, fur hats and fur bags are all very popular and extremely expensive. Manufacturers use the fur from animals such as minks, rabbits, beavers, squirrels, raccoons and many others. Minks make the most expensive fur and for every fur coat, more than fifty minks are killed!

Billions of these animals are killed every year, although today they have mink mills where they breed these animals for their fur.

Since ancient times, tigers, lions, leopards and jaguars have been hunted down – as a game, for their hide and even for their bones. These animals have now reached a point very close to extinction. Most tigers now live in captivity. The Bengal tiger, found in India, Myanmar, Bangladesh and Nepal is an endangered species. There are barely two thousand five hundred Bengal tigers in all four countries. The Bali tiger has already become extinct due to over hunting.

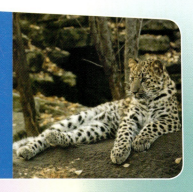

The Amur leopard is critically endangered with very few of its kind remaining in the wild. Other endangered species from the family of big cats are the Snow Leopard, the Wild lions in India, the Barbary lion and the jaguar, besides many others and are all protected species.

Pollution not only affects the health of us humans but that of animals as well. With the coming of industrialization came the need for factories. Factories emit dangerous gases into the air. With the growth of the population and the people's increasing demands, more and more factories are being built each day. Cars and other vehicles also emit dangerous gases into the air. This pollutes the air around us affecting the health and well being of all living organisms.

Water pollution is another factor that contributes to the extinction of living creatures. Oil spills, underground storage leakage, dumping of waste including industrial wastes and radioactive wastes into the water, etc, are all causes of water pollution and causes of the extinction of many marine animals. Frogs are now considered endangered species because of water pollution.

Noise pollution affects animals too. Animals like whales and dolphins that use their sense of hearing for hunting and prey get severely affected, especially with the increased ship traffic.

The hawksbill sea turtle has been hunted for centuries for its shell which is used as a decorative item; it has been used for jewellery, combs and rings and has even been hunted down for food. Today, this animal has fallen into the list of critically endangered species.

The markhor is a large wild goat that has been hunted down famously for sport and game. This creature is endemic to countries like India, Pakistan, Afghanistan, southern Tajikistan and southern Uzbekistan. It is also hunted for food and for its horns. Today, it stands as an endangered species.

Deforestation has destroyed the homes and habitats of many birds too. The Philippine eagle is a critically endangered species and it is believed that there are not more than five hundred of them in Philippines today.

Deforestation, hunting, poaching, competition with other domestic livestock have all contributed to the vulnerability of this animal. The red panda, native to the eastern Himalayas and some parts of China, is said to have a population of 10,000 with its numbers slowly declining.

The red fox was considered extinct in the wild in the year 1980 and all existing animals lived in captivity since then. Years later, these animals have been successfully reintroduced into the wild. In the year 2007, it was estimated that there were 300 red wolves remaining in the world, out of which most are in captive breeding.

Thirty per cent of the earth's area is forest area and therefore steps must be taken for the conservation and preservation of animals and their habitats. Cutting, clearing or destruction of forests should be prevented. Wildlife sanctuaries and national parks can be created for these animals to live.

Activities such as bird watching should be encouraged. Hides can be set up so as to allow people to watch birds from the building without disturbing them.

Whales have been hunted for their meat and oil for centuries. Today, this act has been condemned by many countries and environmental groups and activists. Indeed, if the whale is being hunted down as much as was the dodo or the giant moa, it would soon go their way and become extinct. Thousands of whales are killed every year. Anti-whaling countries have provisions for whale watching, where people get to watch a whale and learn about it at the same time.

The Giant Panda, found only in China is amongst the most threatened animals living today. The government has set up panda reserves all over the country, protecting their habitats and the animals as well. Today, the number of panda's in the country has increased considerably.

INDEX

A

albatrosses 53
alligators 105, 113, 114, 116–118
allosaurus 205
amphibians 59, 131-132
anglerfish 147
antlers 77
ants 188
 army ants 194
apes 63 - 64, 101
arachnids 195 – 197
archaeopteryx 205
archer fish 162
asteroid 208
aye-aye 65

B

babies 21, 59, 86, 103, 123, 166, 175
 chicks 22, 41
babirusa 97
baboons 64
backbone 13, 59, 102, 149, 181
badgers 83
bald eagle 20, 30
barn owls 32
barracuda 160
bats 94–95, 98, 204
bears 78–80, 179
beavers 75, 96, 214
bed bugs 189
bees 79, 188, 190, 191
beetles 188, 194, 196
bird watching 220

birds 13-58, 170–172
 beaks 19, 28, 50, 55, 89, 167, 170, 172, 207, 210
 bills 13, 42, 50, 96
 eggs 18, 21, 22, 36, 41, 57, 61
 feathers 13, 14, 25, 27, 29, 32, 41, 44, 46, 52
 migration 17-18
 nests 19-21, 44
 wings 15, 26, 29, 30, 39, 53
birds of prey 28-30
birth 50, 61, 91, 153, 175
bluebirds 35, 36
boa 118
bones 15, 126, 156, 201, 202, 204
brains 37, 56, 61, 63, 101, 175, 177, 187
budgerigars 48
butterflies 188, 193
 metamorphosis 193

C

camouflage 60, 72, 109
cardinals 36
carnivores 66, 88
caterpillars 193
centipedes 199-200
chameleon 112, 184
cheetah 68
chimpanzee 48, 63
chipmunk 74
clams 183, 184
cleaner shrimp 148
climate change 209, 213
cobra 121, 123
cockatoos 49
cockroach 191

cold-blooded 59, 102, 144
conservation 58, 219
corn snake 120
coyote 72, 83
crabs 153, 182, 183
crane 52, 58
Cretaceous 203, 205, 207
crickets 188, 193
crocodiles 104, 113-117, 164-166
crows 34, 37
cuckoos 18, 21
cuttlefish 184

D

damselfish 160
deforestation 210-213, 218
dinosaurs 143, 201-208
dodos 41, 210
dolphins 40, 89–91, 176–177
dragonflies 188
ducks 22, 42, 44-45, 171

E

eagles 28–30, 57
earthworms 198
echolocation 94
eels 156, 161
elephants 84, 209, 213
emperor penguins 41
endangered 101, 214-218
euoplocephalus 207
extinct 41, 101, 114, 116, 201, 202, 208-211, 213-214, 216, 219, 221

F

falcon 28, 57
ferrets 81
fireflies 194

fish 144-162
    shoal 148
    gills 134, 139, 140, 144, 145, 151, 156, 159, 182
    fins 144, 150, 154, 178
flamingo 51
fleas 189
flightless birds 38-41, 210
flounder 158
fossils 103, 107, 202, 207
foxes 70, 72, 219
frogs 131-138
    life cycle 134-135
fur 60, 64, 72, 79, 81, 82, 179, 214

G
game birds 24-27, 57
gecko 109-110
geese 42-43, 57
giant moa 210
giant panda 101, 221
goldfish 158
gorillas 64
grasshopper 188, 196
grouse 24-25
guinea pigs 101

H
habitat 58, 98, 101, 210, 218, 219, 221
hagfish 149
hammerhead shark 151
hares 57, 73
hawks 28, 29, 57
hawksbill turtles 129, 217
herd 77, 98, 205, 207
herons 51-52
hibernation 102

hippopotamus 84, 85
hooves 76
hornet 191, 192
house fly 190
humming bird 91, 173, 176

I
iguana 108, 166-167
insects 188-193
invertebrates 181-187

J
jaguar 214, 215
jellyfish 181
Jurassic 14, 203, 205

K
kangaroo 86
kelp 82
kingfisher 170
koalas 87
krill 92, 173

L
ladybird 188, 192
lamprey 190
lateral line 149
learning 22, 61, 153, 221
leatherback turtle 129
lemurs 63, 65
leopards 69, 214, 215
lions 67, 97
lizards 104, 106, 108-112, 166-167
lobsters 183, 185
loggerhead turtle 128
lovebirds 47

M
macaw 47
mammals 13, 59-101, 173-179
    birth 61, 91, 153, 175
    brain 61, 63, 101, 175, 177
    hair 89, 60
    migration 98-99
    milk 89
marsupials 86-88, 96
mastodon 209
mercows 93
Mesozoic 203
millipede 200
mite 197
mockingbird 37
mollusc 181, 182, 184
monkeys 63-65, 101
moose 100

N
narwhal 90, 174
newts 131, 132, 141-142
nightingale 35

O
oceans 143-162, 169, 172-179, 181-187
    ocean floor 154, 185
    sea 53-55, 82, 89-93
    sunlight zone 143
octopus 181
oil spills 216
ostriches 38
owls 31-33
oysters 182, 183

P
parasaurolophus 207
parrotfish 159

parrots 46-49
peacocks 27
pelicans 55, 72
penguins 40, 41, 170, 172
pigeons 56
pinnipeds 92, 78
piranha 161
plankton 51, 144, 146
plateosaurus 204
platypus 61, 96
plesiosaurs 204
polar bear 79, 179
pollution 215
   water pollution 216
porcupine 60, 96
porcupine fish 147
porpoises 89, 174, 176-177
possum 87
primates 63-65, 101
pterosaurs 204
puma 69
pygmy owl 33
python 118, 119, 121

Q
quail 24

R
rabbits 73, 101, 214
rats 73, 106
reindeer 98
reptiles 102-130, 163-169
   eggs 103, 105, 106, 115, 123, 127, 128
   scales 102-104, 118, 163, 166
rhinoceros 85
robins 34, 35
rodents 73, 74, 82

S
sabre tooth cat 209
salamanders 131, 132, 133-141
sand dollars 186
scorpions 188, 195, 197
sea anemones 185
sea birds 53-55, 170-172
sea cucumbers 185-186
sea horse 157
sea lions 92, 178
sea otters 82, 179
sea turtles 104, 152, 168-169
seals 92, 152, 174, 178, 179
sharks 150-153
Siamese fighting fish 160
snails 182
snakes 104, 105, 118-123, 167-168
songbirds 34-37
spiders 188, 195-197
spinosaurus 206
spoonbills 50
squid 182
squirrels 214
starfish 185
stink bugs 190
stonefish 156
storks 50
sunstars 186
swallows 34
swans 42

T
tadpole 134-135, 140
tarsiers 63
Tasmanian devil 88
Tasmanian wolf 211
termites 192
thrush 34, 35
ticks 197
tigers 68, 214
toads 131, 133
tortoises 124-125, 168
tree frogs 136
tyrannosaurus rex 206
Triassic 203-205
triceratops 205
tuataras 106-107
tuna 157
turkeys 21, 26
turtles 104, 124-130, 168-169

V
vampire bats 95
velociraptors 14
vertebrates 13-179
vultures 28, 29

W
walrus 92, 93, 178
warm-blooded 13, 59, 102, 173
waterfowl 42-43
weasel 81-83
weaverbirds 19
webs 195, 196
whales 91, 99, 173-177, 216, 221
wobbegong shark 151, 153
wolves 72, 211, 219
wombats 88, 211
worms 198-199

Z
zebra 77
zoos 97, 101, 124